BEEF
IT
UP!

BEEF IT UP!

50 Mouthwatering Recipes for Ground Beef, Steaks, Stews, Roasts, Ribs, and More

Jessica Formicola

Storey Publishing

The mission of Storey Publishing is to serve our customers by publishing practical information that encourages personal independence in harmony with the environment.

Edited by Deanna F. Cook and Lisa H. Hiley
Art direction and book design by Ash Austin
Text production by Jennifer Jepson Smith
Indexed by Andrea Chesman

Cover and interior photography © Dominic Perri
Additional photography by © AlexPro9500/iStock
.com, 16 & 17; Ash Austin © Storey Publishing, LLC,
2; Augustine Wong/Unsplash, vi & 136 (background);
© bigacis/stock.adobe.com, 8; Jason Leung/Unsplash,
3; © laplateresca/stock.adobe.com, 11; © Maksim
Shebeko/stock.adobe.com, 14; Mars Vilaubi © Storey
Publishing, LLC, i, 19–21, 132–134; © Natalia
Lisovskaya/stock.adobe.com, 18; © Xalanx/stock
.adobe.com, 15
Photo styling by Paola Andrea Ramirez
Food styling by Joy Howard
Illustrations © The Bright Agency/Sayada Ramdial, x, 24,
40, 56, 70, 104, 116; Ash Austin © Storey Publishing,
LLC, cover and throughout (cow icon and back-
ground), 5, 10, 12, 13, 22, 23, 123, 126

Text © 2022 by Jessica Formicola

Storey books are available at special discounts when
purchased in bulk for premiums and sales promotions
as well as for fund-raising or educational use. Special
editions or book excerpts can also be created to speci-
fication. For details, please call 800-827-8673, or send
an email to sales@storey.com.

Storey Publishing
210 MASS MoCA Way
North Adams, MA 01247
storey.com

Printed in the United States by Versa Press
10 9 8 7 6 5 4 3 2 1

Library of Congress Cataloging-in-Publication Data
on file

This book is dedicated to my husband, who believes all recipes would taste better with hot sauce and bacon, and to my kids, who still call all types of protein "chicken." Thank you for eating beef nearly every day for 3 months without any complaints.

And to my assistants, Tayler Ross and Holley Stack, who helped me stay sane during the process. And to my parents, in-laws, and sister, who provided unconditional support along the way.

CONTENTS

A BEEF-LOVER'S DREAM COME TRUE

Imagine my delight when, after years of writing about food, I was given the opportunity to write an entire cookbook dedicated to beef. Since my early days as a food blogger, I've been an ambassador for the Certified Angus Beef brand, working with this nonprofit group to educate consumers about beef. They provided me with the opportunity to visit family-owned and family-run cattle ranches, where I was fascinated to learn about the genetics of beef cattle and the cycle of raising beef. Did you know that as many as 100 people and almost 2 years are dedicated to raising an individual cow? I also learned a great deal from professional butchers and chefs, and enjoyed developing recipes of my own.

Once I started working on this book, I quickly realized that I had far more information than pages available. For one thing, there are many more cuts of beef than chicken or pork. And while other proteins might be more easily interchangeable, each cut of beef has its own distinct characteristics and preparation methods. I overwhelmed myself researching the most popular beef dishes, which I had to whittle from 150 to a mere 50. I tried my best to provide myriad flavors and a wide variety of cuts while giving fresh takes on tried-and-true favorites.

These recipes just skim the surface of classic beefy meals. They may remind you of meals that your mom or grandmother prepared or even some old favorites that you had forgotten about. My goal was to bring back some memorable beef dishes but with a modern twist to reflect changes in home-cooking techniques and a greater acceptance of a variety of flavors. That means many of these recipes are associated with specific cultures, although I'm not claiming they are authentic. People often tell me that the Italian dishes I make from handed-down family recipes aren't authentic, and I'm not sure how much more authentic it gets. With this book, I'm simply celebrating beef while embracing the beautiful diversity of cuisines that have influenced me.

And I want to share my passion and knowledge of beef with the home cook. I, too, am a home cook, just one who happens to make beef ALL. THE. TIME. I'm also a full-time working mom and wife. Everyone, even my young children, enjoys a good meal, but we don't always have the time to make that happen.

Through the years I've developed four pillars that I live by in the kitchen: salt, seasonings, sauces, and swaps. Using these pillars means that every meal can be a standout, even if it's just a matter of using the right salt (not all are created equal!) or a spice you may not have thought to add to beef before. Simple sauces can make or break a dish, and the knowledge of how to make easy swaps can save the day when you suddenly realize you're out of balsamic vinegar.

I hope you will use this cookbook to bring beef to your dinner table more often, learn something new, and have a good time cooking.

Jessica Formicella

BEEF UP YOUR
Knowledge

Whether you eat meat every day or just once in a while, beef deserves a place at your table. It's a great source of protein, tastes delicious, and is incredibly versatile, able to take center stage or play a supporting role. But it can be confusing figuring out what the various cuts are, let alone which ones work best with which recipes. Here's a quick introduction to the basics of buying and using beef.

As a postscript, I'm a firm believer that we should understand where our food comes from. Whether you buy your meat directly from a local producer, at a farmers' market or butcher shop, or in the grocery store, take some time to learn about how it gets to your table.

WHAT BEEF SHOULD I BUY?

For many of us, buying chicken or pork is pretty straightforward, but beef presents a medley of confusing choices. So let's begin with a discussion of what you might find for sale. For starters, all beef sold at retail is inspected for safety and wholesomeness by the United States Department of Agriculture (USDA). After a carcass passes inspection, the producer can request that it be graded and (literally) stamped for approval. The different grades of meat are defined as follows.

Prime is the highest quality and accounts for about 9 percent of all beef that is sold. This meat has abundant fat marbling like little snowflakes evenly dispersed through the cut. The high fat content makes for more tender and flavorful cuts.

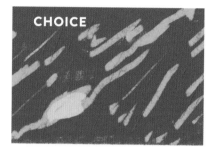

Choice accounts for nearly 75 percent of the meat sold in the United States, making it the most commonly available grade. These cuts have a moderate to modest amount of marbling, offer generous flavor, and are still perfectly juicy.

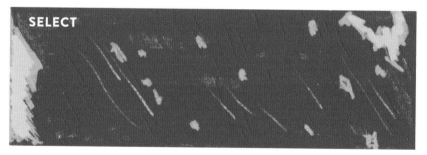

Select meat is leaner and has the least amount of marbling. These cuts tend to need more work in the kitchen to make them flavorful and tender.

Unlabeled beef, also known as "no-roll," does not meet any of the standards above. It ranges in quality but is still perfectly safe to eat and can be prepared in a scrumptious meal.

How Much Fat?

Lean-to-fat ratio. All beef contains fat, although the amount of it varies from cut to cut. Meat that comes from a more muscular part of the animal, such as the shoulders and legs, has less fat, while cuts from the back and loin have more fat. (See page 4 for an explanation of the many different cuts of beef and where they come from.)

Lean means that a 100-gram serving (about 3.5 ounces) contains less than 10 grams of fat and 4.5 grams of saturated fat.

Extra lean means that a 100-gram serving contains less than 5 grams of fat and 2 grams of saturated fat. A ratio of 80/20, which is common for ground beef, means that the meat is 80 percent lean, 20 percent fat.

Marbling refers to the lines and flecks of fat within the individual muscles. The amount of marbling directly impacts the juiciness, flavor, and tenderness of a cut of meat.

CUTS DEMYSTIFIED

Most people know a few beef cuts by name, but they are often unsure which ones are best for a particular recipe or how to best prepare them. The more knowledgeable you are about various cuts, the more you can swap them out depending on what's available and the more reliable your results will be. More information means better cooking!

Simply selecting a piece of meat that looks like the right shape for a particular recipe may not yield the best results. For example, a chuck roast and a bottom round look similar but cook very differently. The same is true with a flat iron and skirt steak, or even

filet mignon and a mock tender steak, which is just a center-cut chuck roast.

Cuts of beef are broken down into two main categories: primal and subprimal. The first thing a butcher does is divide the carcass into eight large sections, based on the area of the body and the function of the muscle. These primal cuts are the shank, brisket, rib, short plate, flank, round, chuck, and loin. Each of these is processed further into subprimal cuts, which are what you see on the label when you buy beef. There are more than 100 subprimal cuts, and the names often vary depending on geography.

PRIMAL CUT	SUBPRIMAL CUTS	DESCRIPTION/NOTES	
Shank	Stew meat, beef shanks (center and cross-cut), lean ground beef	The shank is located on the lower abdomen and leg. Because those muscles are in constant use, the meat is tough and lean, containing an average of 7% fat.	
Brisket	Brisket point and brisket flat (often referred to as "points" and "flats"). The point comes to a tapered end and is a little rounder with more marbling throughout, while the more common flat brisket has a thick layer of fat on top of the meat.	Brisket comes from the lower chest. It is a flat, highly utilized muscle that is fairly lean and will be tough if not prepared correctly.	
Rib	Prime rib or standing rib roast (prized for its marbling and tenderness; expensive, as there are only two per cow), ribeye steak (also pricey), back ribs (less meaty, with a high volume of cartilage)	The large rib section comes from the center back of the animal. These cuts tend to be highly marbled, naturally juicy, and superbly flavored.	

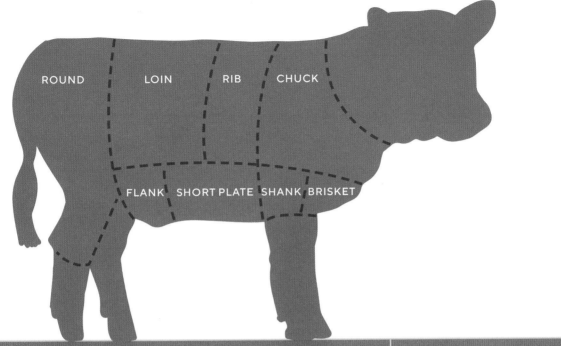

OPTIMAL COOKING METHODS	COMMON USES
Slow and pressure cooking, braising. These cuts tend to require manual tenderizing (with a meat mallet or grinder), marinades to help break down fibers and to impart flavor, and low and slow cooking methods to keep the meat moist.	Stew, soup, osso buco, curry, pot pie
A properly prepared brisket is life changing, but they are known for being challenging. Both cuts require long, moist heat to create succulent bites, therefore moist smoking, slow cooking, and braising are the best methods.	Pastrami, corned beef, BBQ brisket, burnt ends
These cuts require quick, high, and dry heat, whether in the oven, smoker, or on the grill. Prime rib, usually reserved for special occasions, is typically served rare to medium rare with a nice crust. Ribeye steaks are best with a nice sear over fire, in a skillet, or even broiled in the oven. Back ribs are typically dry rubbed and then smoked or grilled.	Steaks, rib roast, BBQ ribs

Continued on next page

PRIMAL CUT	SUBPRIMAL CUTS	DESCRIPTION/NOTES	
Short plate	Short ribs, skirt steak	This section is on the belly directly under the ribs, neighbored by the brisket and flank. These cuts have a higher fat content than the chuck or flank regions, and each requires a different cooking method.	
Flank	Flank steak (a little goes a long way with this cut, making it an economical choice)	Coming from behind the short plate on the belly, this meat is lean, thick, long, and tends to be chewy.	
Round	Sirloin tip, top round, bottom round (rump roast), and eye of round. These lean cuts tend to cost less per pound.	The round comes from the hind quarters. Because the meat contains little collagen, it does best cooked low and slow with added liquid.	
Chuck	Chuck roast (sometimes labeled chuck eye roast, chuck pot roast, mock tender steak, or chuck roll roast), top blade, flat iron, country-style ribs (boneless), shoulder cuts, ground beef	The chuck comes from the shoulder and lower neck. These muscles are highly exercised but still have a good amount of fat and connective tissue. When cooked properly, chuck is amazingly tender. Ground beef from this area is ideal for hamburgers as it is about 20% fat.	
Loin	Top loin, bottom loin, sirloin, and tenderloin, resulting in more than 20 subprimal cuts, depending on the butcher. The most popular are porterhouse, T-bone, filet mignon, New York strip, sirloin steak, chateaubriand (beef tenderloin), and tri-tip, although I find that tri-tips are easier to locate on the West Coast.	The loin section, located on the lower back of the cow, is a low-activity area that produces numerous desirable cuts.	

OPTIMAL COOKING METHODS	COMMON USES
Short ribs are best prepared using a pressure cooker, braising, or smoking. Skirt steaks are thin, can be marinated or rubbed, and are best cooked with a sear.	Recipes calling for thin strips of meat: stir-fries, fajitas, sandwiches, pasta dishes
Flank steak needs manual tenderizing or a long stint in a highly acidic marinade to break down fibers. It can be cut thinly and against the grain, which shortens fibers and makes it easier to chew. Preferred cooking methods are prepared on the grill or broiled in the oven.	Recipes calling for thicker strips of meat: salads, pasta dishes, tacos, sandwiches
Braising, pressure cooker methods, and roasting tend to work best. These cuts aren't very flavorful, but with careful marinating, seasoning, and a good gravy or sauce, they can become showstoppers.	Philly cheesesteaks, pot roast, roast beef
Versatile and easy to prepare, chuck roasts are ideal for long, slow cooking methods that result in a rich, tender dish. A top blade is a roast with a tendon running down the center. Cutting along the tendon produces two blade steaks; cutting in the opposite direction results in two flat iron steaks. The top blade section is one of the tastiest cuts, requiring just a bit of seasoning and a quick sear over high heat.	Pot roast, chicken-fried steak, cube steak, BBQ ribs, shredded beef
With between 20 and 30% fat and varying levels of marbling, these cuts require little preparation and quick, dry heat sources such as a grill or hot skillet to produce mouthwatering results.	Filet mignon, beef Wellington, grilled or seared steaks, kabobs, skillet meals requiring tender meat that cooks quickly

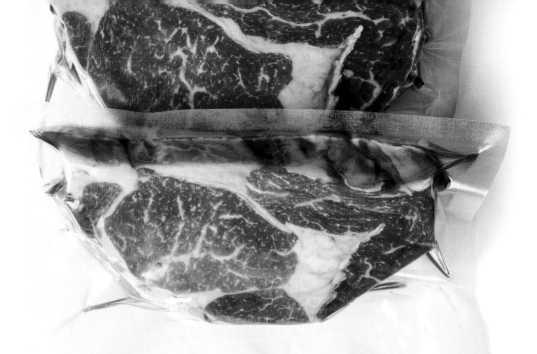

SHOPPING GUIDELINES

Fresh beef should typically be cooked and consumed within 5 days of being packaged; otherwise, it should be frozen. Most beef is sent to stores as larger cuts, which are then broken down for sale. Some cuts may be frozen for future demand; for example, prime rib is more popular around holidays. Most stores label meat with either a "packaged on" or a "sell by" date, which is later than the packaging date, but there is no federal mandate to do so. Be mindful of which date is on the package and treat the meat accordingly.

Here are a few more tips for selecting beef.

Check for "good" fat. Depending on the cut, look for intramuscular marbling, meaning flecks of fat present throughout the piece of meat. Seam fat, also known as intermuscular fat, is the thicker, solid layer on the edge of a steak or other cut. Depending on the recipe, you might be asked to trim this before cooking, but you can also use this fat to baste and flavor during the cooking process and then carve it off before serving.

Pay attention to the color. Freshly butchered beef is a deep burgundy color. Vacuum-sealed beef that was packaged directly after processing might be close to this color. Within a few minutes, however, oxidization and chemical changes in the myoglobin cause the meat to become the bright red you usually see at a store. After a few days, the meat will turn grayish brown. This doesn't necessarily mean that the beef is spoiled, but it should be used or frozen soon. Changes in color are normal.

Look for liquid. The blood is drained from the carcass before butchering, so any red juice in the packaging is water combined with proteins. It is harmless but indicates that the package has been in the meat case long enough for the meat to have lost moisture.

Take a whiff. Meat with a funky smell might be nearing the end of its safe window for consumption. And while it isn't possible to touch meat before buying it, if you have beef at home that has a tacky or slimy surface, toss it.

STORAGE AND HANDLING

When you've made your selection, place the package of beef in a plastic bag, usually provided at the meat counter, to catch leaks and prevent potential cross contamination to other foods as you transport it. As much as possible, avoid letting it sit at room temperature. Keep meat cool by placing it with other cold-storage items in insulated bags or a cooler in your car and put it in the refrigerator as soon as you can.

According to the USDA, for the safety of all foods, refrigerators should maintain a temperature lower than 40°F (4°C), with an ideal holding temperature of 38°F (3°C). Anything above 40°F (4°C) is considered the "danger zone" where pathogens that cause foodborne illnesses can grow. Do not allow beef to sit out of the refrigerator for more than 2 hours before cooking. (See The Myth of Room-Temperature Meat, page 11.)

Meat should be stored in its original packaging, in a plastic bag or airtight container to catch possible leaks. Keep it on the bottom shelf and toward the back, where the temperature is the coldest and isn't as affected by the opening and closing of the doors.

Beef does not need to be rinsed before cooking. Any bacteria present on exterior surfaces will be killed during the cooking process.

Prepare or cut raw meat on nonporous cutting boards designated for raw foods. Use a separate board to slice cooked meat. Clean all utensils and cutting boards with hot water and soap and allow to fully air-dry before storing.

Freezing Beef

Beef that is within 5 days of being packaged can be safely frozen for up to 12 months in a standard freezer and even longer in a chest freezer, where the temperature is more stable. The key to having it turn out just as delicious as it was going in is to package it correctly.

If the original packaging is butcher paper or plastic wrap, or if the meat has been vacuum sealed, you can freeze it as is for up to 3 months in a standard freezer. For long-term freezing, the ideal solution is to remove it from the paper or plastic wrap and to vacuum seal it. If you do not own a vacuum sealer, the next best option is to tightly wrap the original package in freezer paper or aluminum foil to prevent freezer burn. Label each package with the cut and weight and the date it went into the freezer.

Storing Ground Beef

Ground beef is a bit of an exception to other cuts, as the process of grinding exposes exponentially more surface area, which increases the probability that any ground meat carries bacteria. Ground beef should always be stored in the back of the refrigerator, used within 3 days of packaging, and be cooked to no less than 160°F (71°C). This applies to meatballs, hamburgers, meatloaf, and anything else that uses ground beef.

Ground beef is also less freezer friendly and more susceptible to freezer burn than other cuts. It should be vacuum sealed or wrapped tightly in freezer paper or aluminum foil and used within 6 months.

Defrosting Beef

Freezing meat at 0°F (–17°C) or lower successfully inactivates some food bacteria, but these can grow if the meat is not properly thawed or handled after freezing. The best way to defrost meat is to allow it to slowly increase in temperature up to 40°F (4°C). Because meat should not be held above that temperature for any length of time, the safest ways to defrost it are in the refrigerator or in cold water. But as a busy mom of two, I understand that planning in advance doesn't always happen. In a beef emergency (we've all needed a last-minute hamburger, right?), you can use the defrost function of your microwave.

Refrigerator method. This method requires planning ahead as it takes the longest. Steaks, ground beef, and thinner roasts will thaw in 24 hours or less, but larger cuts of meat, especially those with bones, might take 2 to 3 days.

Cold-water method. Cold water works faster but still requires time. A larger roast will take several hours to fully defrost. If the meat isn't already in an airtight plastic bag, transfer it to one (vacuum-sealed packaging is watertight). Run the water from the tap to get it really cold, then fill a container or even the sink itself. Submerge the meat, changing the water every 30 to 40 minutes to keep it at 40°F (4°C) or below until the cut of meat is fully thawed. A large roast is like a giant ice cube and will keep the water cold at first, but you'll need to change the water more often closer to the end of defrosting.

Microwave method. The defrost function on a microwave will safely increase the internal temperature of your meat but use this method only in a pinch and only if you plan to cook the meat immediately after thawing it. Keep a close eye to be sure the meat is thawing, not cooking. Meat cooked in a microwave tends to be rubbery and chewy. If you do not have a defrost function, zap the meat on 50 percent power at 1-minute intervals, flipping it over in between, until thawed.

What not to do. It may be tempting to fill the sink with hot water and throw the meat in to let it thaw like an ice cube, but that's not worth the risk. Using hot water or leaving meat out on the counter to thaw allows the surface area of the meat to become the perfect breeding ground for bacteria while the center is still frozen. Hot water can also begin to cook the outer layer, which will compromise your recipe later.

DEFROSTING TECHNIQUES

In the Refrigerator
Takes from 24 hours up to 3 days

In Cold Water
Takes several hours

In the Microwave
Takes a few minutes, with care

In Hot Water
DO NOT DO THIS!
Cooks the outer layer while leaving the center frozen

Dealing with Freezer Burn

Freezer burn occurs when moisture is released and oxygen is introduced into a poorly wrapped package. It creates icy spots on the meat that may turn gray and have a leathery appearance. Freezer-burned meat, although unsightly, is safe to eat, but the taste and texture will be significantly altered. You can cut away smaller spots, but I suggest discarding a piece of meat if the whole thing is affected.

The Myth of Room-Temperature Meat

I can't tell you how many times I've read a recipe that says to "bring the meat to room temperature" or heard people say they always let meat sit on the counter for 20 minutes before throwing it on the grill so as not to "shock it." While it's true that the goal is to have the meat be a consistent temperature throughout before you cook it, problems arise when a cut of meat has drastically different temperatures in different parts.

For example, a strip steak might be thawed on the exterior but still frozen on the interior. Because of the difference, it will not cook evenly: When the outside is properly cooked, the inside might not even be warm. Meat that is properly thawed to an internal temperature of 40°F (4°C), as described on the facing page, could take several more hours to come to room temperature depending on the size and thickness of the cut. However, the FDA recommends that meat not sit out longer than 2 hours before being cooked, and no longer than 1 hour after being cooked before being refrigerated again.

OVERVIEW OF COOKING METHODS

With many options for cuts of beef also come many options for cooking beef. Some cuts lend themselves to specific preparation methods, while others are completely versatile.

 **Air frying** is achieved using a small convection oven that circulates highly heated air around food. The result is similar to deep-frying without submerging the food in oil. This method is best for smaller steaks that are uniform in size or for baked appetizers. It also happens to be my favorite way to reheat nearly any dish!

 **Frying and stir-frying** are quick-heat methods using a small amount of oil in a skillet or pan on the stovetop. Quick pan sears like this are best for thinner cuts or steaks prepared to a medium degree (or under) of doneness. Panfrying is also a way to brown meat and ground beef and might be combined with another method, such as braising, stewing, or roasting.

 Braising is a form of moist-heat cooking mostly used with larger roasts. The meat is partially submerged in a liquid base flavored with a splash of acid, seasonings, herbs, or even veggies, then cooked low and slow. The process allows connective tissues and collagen time to melt, making typically tougher cuts tender. This can be done in the oven, on the stovetop, or in a slow cooker.

 **Grilling** produces unmistakable flavor and char from the open flame. Cooking with dry heat is best for naturally tender steaks that aren't too thick. Larger cuts that require longer, steady temperatures tend to do better with smoking.

 **Broiling** is an excellent swap if you don't have a grill. Nothing replaces the undeniable flavors of a real fire but cooking a piece of meat inches from the oven's heating element comes close. This method works best for thinner and uniformly shaped cuts.

 **Pressure cooking** has regained popularity, and there is a good reason why. This method cooks foods in liquid in amazingly fast times while keeping them supermoist and helping to break down fibers. It works best for tougher cuts of beef.

Roasting is applying extended dry heat, with the total time depending on the size of the cut and desired degree of doneness. The process commonly starts or ends with a higher temperature to create a bark, or crust, on the exterior. This is similar to browning but done in the oven rather than separately.

Slow cooking is essentially the same process as braising or even stewing, but in a countertop appliance that maintains a consistent and precise low temperature. The moisture stays locked inside the pot, allowing for all the natural juices to become the braising/stewing liquid.

Stewing is similar to braising but in general applies to smaller pieces of meat that are fully submerged in liquid. The smaller pieces typically need less cooking time to become fork-tender than a large roast.

Let's Talk about Browning

Browning is probably the most overlooked and under-appreciated technique in cooking. Any chef will tell you it is one of the best tricks in the bag for developing flavor with little seasoning other than the naturally occurring notes caused by heat. Browning works with meat, vegetables, fruit, nearly any grain or nut, and even dairy (who doesn't love browned butter?). It is also the most commonly ignored step in a recipe, but here's a word to the wise: *Do not skip this step!*

The technical term for browning is the Maillard reaction, named after Louis-Camille Maillard, the scientist who discovered the chemical reaction that occurs when high heat is applied to food. The process changes the structure of certain amino acids and sugars, causing them to rearrange in rings and to create changes in color and flavor.

While most commonly thought of in connection with meats and other proteins, the Maillard reaction happens in all types of cooking—including baking, sautéing, even toasting marshmallows. It is not achieved through methods such as braising, slow cooking, or pressure cooking, so browning is typically done before a second cooking method is undertaken. In some cases, it is done after a slower cooking process to create a reverse sear.

Browning How-Tos

Dry the meat by patting it with a paper towel or even letting it sit uncovered in the refrigerator for a while. Smaller cuts might need only 1 or 2 hours, but larger roasts can sit overnight. It is difficult to get good color on wet meat.

Next, add some seasoning. In the case of beef, this almost always includes salt. Salt brings out the natural flavors and helps create a nice bark—that's the char on the outside of a cooked steak or roast. It can be naturally flavored or incorporate herbs and spices.

Preheat your cooking vessel. More often than not, home cooks don't set the heat high enough to sufficiently dehydrate the outer layer for the Maillard reaction—the browning—to occur. You need to use medium-high to high heat (375 to 450°F/190 to 230°C). Placing the meat in a cold pan and allowing it to heat up won't produce good results.

When you put the meat in the sizzling-hot pan, make sure the pieces have room to breathe. If you're browning steaks or smaller cuts, don't pack them in like sardines.

After the meat hits the pan, allow it to sit long enough for the moisture to evaporate and the outside to sear. Moving it around too frequently prevents this from happening. Generally speaking, the reaction will occur within 3 to 4 minutes, after which you can turn each piece of beef and continue until the whole piece is nicely browned. Steaks will need only one flip if seared properly.

GROUND BEEF

How many recipes tell you to "brown and drain" ground beef? Many, including some in this book. However, if meat is browned at too low a heat, it ends up dry, rubbery, and gray. Just like other cuts, ground beef should be browned on high heat, cooking it hot and fast to develop deep umami flavors while retaining natural moisture.

Start by putting the entire amount of meat in one piece in the hot pan. Let it sit in the pan to develop a good char on one side, then flip it over and allow the other side to brown nicely as well, about 3 minutes per side.

Once the entire amount is well browned, break it into pieces and stir until all traces of pink are gone, which will depend greatly on the amount of beef and size of the pan. Drain off any liquid that collects during the process, as too much liquid can prevent browning.

Not crowding the pan applies to ground beef as much as to other cuts. If the pan just fits a thick layer of beef, the meat ends up steaming instead of searing. Work in batches if necessary, and make sure the meat has enough room for air to circulate and steam to escape.

The leaner the ground beef is, the more important it is to use a high, quick sear to minimize the loss of moisture, or to cook it with liquid to avoid a rubbery texture. If a recipe does call for a low and slow cooking of ground beef, which is different from browning, try adding a small amount of low-sodium beef broth to the pan so you are retaining moisture while adding flavor.

Degrees of Doneness

Beef tartare is served raw and chilled, but most people like their meat at least somewhat cooked. Degrees of doneness, which refer to the internal temperature of cooked beef, progress in this order: rare, medium rare, medium, medium well, and well done. Different cuts and sizes are considered "done" at different temperatures, unlike chicken, which is typically cooked to the same temperature across the board. For example, a rare steak can be served as low as 125°F (52°C) while a roast or brisket might reach 160°F (971°C) or higher.

One of my mentors, Chef Tony Biggs, once told me he would never be responsible for a piece of beef cooked beyond medium doneness (145–149°F/63–65°C), and I tend to agree with him. After this temperature range, the fibers begin to shrink and dry out, becoming chewy and undesirable. That said, some cuts, such as a brisket, require higher heat and longer cooking times for the collagen to start breaking down.

Of course, personal preference plays a part. My college roommate swore that she disliked beef until I finally coaxed her to try some I'd prepared. Turns out her family cooked any cut of beef into chewy, dry oblivion—no wonder she didn't care for it! After experimenting with properly cooked dishes, she found she prefers her meat to be fairly rare and tender and has never looked back.

Degrees of Doneness
These descriptions are useful for steaks, burgers, and some roasts.

DEGREE OF DONENESS	APPEARANCE		INTERNAL TEMPERATURE
Rare	Cool red center		125°F (52°C)
Medium rare	Warm red center		135°F (57°C)
Medium	Warm pink center		145°F (63°C)
Medium well	Slightly pink center		150°F (65°C)
Well done	Little to no pink		160°F (71°C)

How to Tell If Meat Is Cooked Properly

Although color is a good indicator, it should never be substituted for a meat thermometer. Some cuts must reach a specific internal temperature while others can be prepared to your preference, but because cuts of beef vary in thickness and weight, using an instant-read thermometer is the best way to gauge doneness. After all, you don't want to be cutting open an almost perfectly grilled ribeye to see if it's done, only to watch a lot of tasty juices drip away.

Some folks swear they can judge doneness by touch, but results can vary depending on the cut, tension of fibers, and cooking method. And if you are developing a crust, the exterior will be rough and ridged anyhow. After making the same dish over and over, you may learn to tell doneness by giving the meat a quick pinch, but for the average home cook, a thermometer is the only way to gauge doneness accurately and safely.

The reading is taken from the tip of the probe, so you need to insert it toward the center of the meat to find the lowest temperature. Place the thermometer in the thickest part of the beef, away from fat or bone. It should enter at least a half inch into a steak or several inches if you are checking a roast.

I prefer to use a digital instant-read thermometer, but a Wi-Fi–enabled or probe thermometer is also a good option. These models constantly monitor the temperature and sometimes even have built-in alarms to alert you when the roast has completed cooking.

If using an instant-read thermometer, check the temperature halfway through the cooking time and more frequently toward the end. Remove smaller steaks, cuts, and burgers from the heat when the thermometer reads 5°F (–15°C) lower than the desired finished temperature to account for carryover cooking (see page 18). Remove larger roasts from the heat when the thermometer reads 10°F (–12°C) lower than the desired temperature.

Check Your Oven

In addition to taking the temperature of the meat, make sure your oven is properly calibrated so you know the heat is steady and reaching the correct temperature. There are two ways to do this. The easiest is using an inexpensive oven thermometer that can live in the oven, usually hanging from a rack. When checking for temperature accuracy, place the thermometer right in the middle on the center rack, where most food is cooked. Preheat the oven to 350°F (180°C), then compare with the read on the thermometer. If you are concerned about hot or cold spots, place the thermometer in those locations and check them as well.

If you have a Wi-Fi–enabled or probe thermometer, preheat the oven, then open the door and hold the thermometer inside to check the temperature. This method isn't as reliable as using an oven thermometer because you have to open the door, which brings down the temperature.

Whichever approach you choose, be sure to check for temperature accuracy every 3 to 6 months.

Carryover Cooking

Resting the meat for a period of time after it comes off the heat is an important element in proper cooking. That's because the internal temperature continues to rise from retained heat, a phenomenon called carryover cooking. Smaller cuts increase in temperature just a few degrees, whereas large roasts rise in the double digits. Albeit small, the increase is enough to move a rosy-pink steak to the brown zone.

Trust me on this: No matter how tempted you are by that tantalizing aroma, let the meat rest for the appropriate time. You will thank me, I promise.

Resting also allows for the juices to reabsorb into the fibers rather than seeping into a puddle on the cutting board or plate, leaving behind dry, chewy meat. Have you ever noticed your steak at a high-end restaurant pooling? No. That's because it was rested before being presented to you.

If you're saying, "But I don't want my meat to get cold" (I'm looking at you, Mom), don't worry. Your meal will still be hot when you dive in. A large roast resting for up to 20 minutes won't even come to room temperature, let alone be too cool to eat.

If you are still concerned, tent the meat with aluminum foil to trap some of the heat. Make sure it is loosely tented though, not tightly wrapped, or you risk steaming the meat and cooking it even further.

Food Safety

As with any food, proper handling is imperative to ensure that you enjoy food safely. Beef is a unique meat in that it is cooked at a variety of temperatures, sometimes even served raw, even though the USDA recommends that every piece be cooked to a minimum internal temperature of 145°F (63°C) for steaks and roasts, which is about medium, and 160°F (71°C) for ground beef mixtures.

Refer to the Degrees of Doneness chart (page 16) for more specific guidance, and remember to factor in carryover cooking (above) when determining if a cut of meat is properly cooked.

SALT IS THE KEY SEASONING

A superior cut such as filet mignon or prime rib can almost stand on its own when it comes to flavor, needing just some salt and pepper. Other cuts need a bit of enhancing to bring out their best flavor. Herbs that pair well with beef include basil, bay leaf, cilantro, chives, oregano, parsley, rosemary, sage, and tarragon. But no matter which other herbs and spices you are using in a recipe, salt should always be on the list. Along with seasonings, sauces, and swaps, it is one of my four pillars for successful cooking. And I will admit to being a little obsessed with it (see A Quick Guide to Finishing Salts, page 20).

Salt is probably the only ingredient that is used across all cuisines and in just about every method of cooking. The first thing to know is that not all salt is created equal. Salts vary in strength of saltiness, aftertaste, size of the crystals, and how long the crystals take to dissolve. Different types are used for different purposes and sometimes called for at specific points in the cooking process.

The size of the crystals is perhaps the most important factor, because it impacts overall volume. One teaspoon of a fine sea salt or table salt delivers far more saltiness than 1 teaspoon of regular or coarse kosher salt. Rate of solubility is also important. In a marinade, the salt has plenty of time to dissolve, but in something like a quick sauce, you want the salt to dissolve fast and not leave behind a gritty texture.

There are three types of salt I would suggest for every kitchen, but I encourage you to experiment with different ones and to become familiar with the amounts that work in various recipes.

Fine sea salt. Also called table salt (not the iodized kind), it has small, even grains that dissolve quickly. It has a clean aftertaste and is used for seasoning during cooking or when the salt needs to disperse well, as in a sauce.

Coarse kosher salt. The uneven grains have a milder flavor and less sodium by volume than table salt. With medium solubility, it is good for cooking but can also be used as a finishing salt to add texture. In my opinion, kosher salt is the most versatile due to its middle-of-the-road solubility, size of grain, and salty taste. Different brands offer different sized grains. For example, Diamond Crystal is widely used in commercial kitchens due to its medium grains and clean taste. Morton's Coarse Kosher has larger grains and a clean, less "salty" flavor. Experiment with different brands to find your own favorites and learn how to adjust the volume of salt in various recipes.

Finishing salts. These coarse-grained salts are the secret weapon of seasoning, used at the end of cooking to add flavor, color, and texture. There are many types, varying in shape, color, and flavor, but all have low solubility.

A Quick Guide to Finishing Salts

Black. This pitch-black salt comes from areas with volcanic eruptions in both the Pacific Ocean near Hawaii and the Mediterranean Sea near Cyprus. It is gritty and gives a less salty, more umami finish that is excellent on a grilled or panfried steak.

Pink Himalayan. Perfect for tacos and salads, this salt is mined near the Himalayan mountains. It comes in different grain sizes; finely ground, it can substitute in cooking for fine salt. Some believe it has health benefits from trace elements, but I just like that it is pretty, provides crunch, and has a mild salt flavor.

Maldon sea salt. These large, pyramid-shaped crystals make this the perfect salt for lightly finishing nearly any recipe in this book. This is my most favorite salt—I even carry a tin of it in my purse.

Sel gris. This beautiful gray salt from France has a fine, dainty texture. It can be used in place of Maldon and is nicest with foods that will contrast its lovely color.

Swaps and Substitutions

Even the best stocked kitchen and most prepared cook will sometimes run short of an ingredient. Here are some easy ways to fill in the gaps without having to run to the store.

INGREDIENT	INSTEAD
Black pepper	Use an equal amount **white pepper** or one quarter the amount of **cayenne pepper**.
Dijon mustard	Substitute the same amount of **another variety of mustard**. 1 tablespoon prepared mustard equals **1 teaspoon dry mustard plus 1–2 teaspoons vinegar**.
Dried or fresh herbs	The general swap is 1 teaspoon of a **dried herb** for 1 tablespoon of minced **fresh herbs**.
Fresh garlic	1 garlic clove equals ½ teaspoon **granulated garlic** OR ⅛ teaspoon **garlic powder**.
Kosher salt	Use half the amount of **table salt** or **fine sea salt**.
Low-sodium beef broth I use this in all recipes so I can manually adjust the salt levels in a dish. The level of saltiness varies greatly between brands.	Use **regular beef broth** and omit additional salt in the recipe, or use **water** or **wine**.
Onion	1 small onion equals 1 teaspoon **onion powder** OR 1 tablespoon **dried minced onion**.
Unsalted butter	Use **regular butter** but omit additional salt in the recipe.
Worcestershire sauce This rich, fermented sauce pairs particularly well with beef. It's made with vinegar, anchovies, molasses, tamarind, onion, garlic, and other seasonings. A little goes a long way.	Use an equal amount **balsamic vinegar** OR an equal amount **soy sauce plus a pinch of sugar**.
Wine	Substitute an equal amount of **broth** or **water**.

GO-TO KITCHEN TOOLS

Cooking beef may involve a variety of methods, but you don't need a ton of fancy equipment to achieve great results. You probably have everything you need already, but here are some of the kitchen implements that I rely on the most when cooking.

Cast-iron or other heavy-duty skillet. A good-quality pan retains and evenly distributes heat and is heatproof both on the stovetop and in the oven. A well-made cast-iron skillet will last you a lifetime and may even become a cherished family heirloom. Have one that is large enough to hold the amount of meat you typically cook.

Dutch oven. Dutch ovens are large, thick-walled cooking vessels with lids that can be used on the stovetop and in the oven. Good ones are made of cast iron, ceramic, or heavy aluminum. They come in many sizes, but one that holds 9 or 10 quarts is essential for braising large roasts or making stews and soups.

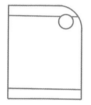

Cutting boards. Keep two sets of cutting boards, one for raw meat and another for produce. I prefer nonporous plastic or glass boards that are easy to clean. Some people use wood boards, claiming that wood has great antimicrobial properties, but I find it hard to get them fully dried out and they require more maintenance. Replace cutting boards after they become scratched up.

Good knives. Make sure you have a set of good-quality knives and learn how to sharpen them. A dull knife is one of the least safe items in the kitchen. A 6-inch chef's knife can do most things from trimming meat to chopping vegetables. I highly recommend having a carving knife for serving larger roasts and making uniform thin slices.

Seasoning Cast Iron

Always season a new cast-iron pan even if the package says "preseasoned," and season it again any time you use more than water to clean it. To season cast iron, wash the pan and dry it well, then wipe on a thin layer of flaxseed, soybean, vegetable, or canola oil. Bake at 350°F (180°C) for an hour and allow to cool in the oven. You can usually clean cast iron by rinsing with plenty of hot water and using coarse salt to scrub off stuck-on food. Dry thoroughly with a towel and apply a thin coating of oil after each use. If you do need to use soap, season the pan in the oven again.

 **Long-handled fork.** These are useful not just for serving but also for flipping roasts and steaks.

 **Meat chopper.** Also called a masher or smasher, this utensil is useful for breaking apart ground beef at the last stage of browning, but it isn't a necessity unless you make a lot of ground beef. A spatula or wire potato masher will work just as well.

 Mini food processor. One of my most-used kitchen tools is a dishwasher-safe mini food processor. I use it to mince garlic and onion, chop veggies, whisk together dressing and sauces, and smooth out soups.

 Mixing bowls. Whether you are using them for prep work, marinating ingredients, or storing leftovers, mixing bowls are a must-have in any kitchen. Glass ones are sturdy, nonporous, and don't have reactive properties like metal, so I find them to be the best all-purpose choice.

 **Rimmed baking sheets.** Inexpensive ones are flimsy and warp when under high heat like the broiler. For a true workhorse in the kitchen, invest in a food-service-grade model made of 18 mm aluminum.

 **Roasting pan.** Larger roasts can be cooked in the bottom of a broiler pan, but a proper roasting pan is sturdier. The higher sides prevent the meat from sliding around and the cooking liquid from splashing out but aren't so high that steam forms.

 **Tongs.** Both short-handled and long-handled tongs are crucial in the kitchen. I prefer the kind with no rubber tips for better handling. Shorter versions give better control when working in a skillet, but longer are best for the grill to stay safely away from the fire. Tongs also won't pierce the meat and release the juices.

BEEFY
Small
Bites

I love to entertain and while beef is typically thought of as a main entrée ingredient, it almost always makes an appearance on my appetizer spread too. Its versatility and quick cooking time puts it in the running for outstanding savory starters worthy of a special occasion or a friendly get-together. Plus, I'm pretty sure I'm not the only one who could happily eat a whole meal of just appetizers. With a few of these protein-packed snacks and a nice salad, you're all set!

Spicy Hand Pies

Spicy hand pies can be served as an appetizer, a snack, side, or even an entrée. These stuffed pastry half-moons can be savory or sweet, and versions of them are found in many cuisines. One of the most traditional preparations is ground beef, veggies, and warm spices.

My family likes food that makes sweat pop on their foreheads, but you can prepare a milder version by omitting the hot peppers.

PREP TIME | 15 minutes   **COOK TIME** | 35 minutes   **MAKES** | 16 hand pies

1 tablespoon vegetable oil
1 pound 80% lean ground beef
½ cup minced white onion
¼ cup minced carrot
¼ cup minced celery
2 garlic cloves, minced
½ cup low-sodium beef broth
⅓ cup frozen peas
1 teaspoon dried oregano
1 teaspoon ground cumin
½ teaspoon chili powder
1 tablespoon white vinegar
½ teaspoon kosher salt
½ teaspoon freshly ground black pepper
1 tablespoon chopped jalapeño or habanero chile (optional)
½ teaspoon red pepper flakes (optional)
1 egg
1 tablespoon water
16 empanada wrappers (see Cook's Note)
Fresh Herb Sauce (page 133)

1. Preheat the oven to 375°F (190°C). Line a large baking sheet with parchment paper.

2. Heat the oil in a large skillet over high heat. Add the beef and allow to brown on one side before breaking apart with a spatula or ground meat chopper. Flip and repeat until no pink remains, 5 to 6 minutes. Remove and drain. Return the meat to the skillet.

3. Add the onion, carrot, celery, and garlic, and cook for 2 to 3 minutes, or until the onion starts to soften and turn opaque. Stir in the broth, peas, oregano, cumin, and chili powder. Mix well, and reduce the heat to low. Simmer until no liquid remains, about 12 minutes.

4. Remove the skillet from the heat and season the meat with the vinegar, salt, black pepper, and the jalapeño and/or red pepper flakes, if using.

5. Whisk the egg and water in a small bowl. Lay out an empanada wrapper and place 2 heaping tablespoons of filling in the center. Brush egg wash on the edges and fold to form a half-moon. Crimp the edge all around like a dumpling, using the tines of a fork or pinching with your fingers. Continue with the remaining wrappers. Baste the top of each hand pie with more egg wash.

6. Bake for 12 minutes, or until lightly browned. Let cool slightly (the filling is hot!), and serve with the herb sauce.

AIR FRYER METHOD

Preheat an air fryer to 350°F (180°C) and spray the fryer basket with cooking spray. Follow the recipe through step 4; in step 5, instead of basting with egg wash, lightly spray each hand pie with cooking spray. Cook for 10 minutes, turning halfway through, until both sides are golden brown.

Cook's Note | Preformed empanada wrappers can be found in the frozen food aisle, but a batch of piecrust also works. Roll out the dough and cut out 4- to 5-inch disks using a round cookie cutter or small bowl.

Sweet & Sour Meatballs

A fusion of cocktail meatballs with the sweet-and-sour sauce we love at Asian restaurants, this recipe quickly became a family favorite. My husband asked me to test it several times "just to be sure it was perfect." The sauce is a little more sour than sweet, with a velvety texture that complements many other dishes.

Simmer a batch in a slow cooker for parties or make a full meal by serving the meatballs with rice and sautéed bell peppers, onions, pineapple chunks, and broccoli. It might seem a little odd, but peaches are also a great addition.

PREP TIME	10 minutes	COOK TIME	50 minutes	MAKES	20 meatballs

FOR THE MEATBALLS

- 1 pound 80% lean ground beef
- 1 egg, lightly beaten
- ¼ cup plain breadcrumbs
- 1 garlic clove, finely minced
- ⅓ cup finely minced white onion
- ½ teaspoon kosher salt

FOR THE SAUCE

- 1½ cups water
- ½ cup firmly packed light brown sugar
- ½ cup ketchup
- ¼ cup white vinegar
- ¼ cup low-sodium soy sauce
- ½ teaspoon ground ginger
- 3 tablespoons cornstarch
  Sesame seeds, for garnish (optional)
  Sliced scallions, for garnish (optional)

1 **Make the meatballs:** Preheat the oven to 350°F (180°C). Coat a 9- by 13-inch baking dish with cooking spray.

2 Crumble the beef into a medium bowl. Toss with the egg, breadcrumbs, garlic, onion, and salt. Roll into 1¾-inch balls, placing them in the prepared baking dish. You should have about 20 meatballs. Bake for 20 minutes, then set aside.

3 **Make the sauce:** Combine 1¼ cups of the water, the sugar, ketchup, vinegar, soy sauce, and ginger in a medium saucepan over medium heat. Whisk until smooth. Reduce heat to low and bring to a simmer.

4 Meanwhile, whisk the cornstarch and remaining ¼ cup water in a small bowl until smooth. Pour this paste into the sauce, stirring until combined. Simmer until the sauce thickens, becomes a deep brown, and is glossy, then continue to cook over low heat for 3 to 4 minutes to reduce by a third.

5 **Finish the dish:** Drain and discard any liquids or excess fat from the meatballs. Add the meatballs to the sauce. Simmer for 25 minutes over medium heat, stirring every 5 minutes.

6 Garnish with the sesame seeds and scallions, if desired.

Freezer Friendly: Store in an airtight container for up to 3 months.

Cook's Notes | Restaurants use food coloring to make their sauce that classic pink. Homemade versions are more brown in color.

To sweeten the sauce, substitute 1 cup pineapple juice for 1 cup water.

You can substitute an equal amount of flour for cornstarch, but the cornstarch gives the sauce a nice glossiness.

Delish Beef Knishes

Knishes remind me of a warm New York City deli on a cold winter day. These little packets of comfort food, similar to Polish pierogi, may seem daunting to make but are actually quite easy. Instead of using the more traditional caramelized onions, which can take an hour all by themselves, I opt for the subtle flavor and fresh crunch of sautéed leeks. I use plain mashed potatoes so as not to overpower the beef, but you can jazz them up with garlic or a bit of sour cream if you like.

But the filling is really all about the meat. This is the ideal recipe for using up leftovers such as pot roast beef (page 81), shredded beef (page 72), or even a fancy tenderloin (page 118).

PREP TIME | 20 minutes   **COOK TIME** | 30 minutes   **MAKES** | 24 knishes

1 tablespoon unsalted butter

2 leeks, white parts only, thinly sliced

1 cup cooked mashed potatoes, cooled

4 ounces cream cheese, softened

1½ cups cooked beef, chopped or shredded into 1-inch pieces

½ cup shredded cheddar cheese

1 teaspoon hot sauce

2 tablespoons milk

1 teaspoon garlic powder

½ teaspoon kosher salt

½ teaspoon freshly ground black pepper

2 (11-ounce) packages prepared bread dough

1 egg

2 tablespoons water

2 teaspoons poppy or sesame seeds (optional)

1. Preheat the oven to 350°F (180°C). Line a large rimmed baking sheet with parchment paper.

2. Melt the butter in a medium skillet over low heat, then add the leeks. Cook until soft and slightly browned, about 10 minutes.

3. Combine the potatoes and cream cheese in a medium bowl. Stir in the beef, cheese, hot sauce, milk, garlic powder, salt, and pepper.

4. Stretch each package of bread dough into a 4- by 16-inch rectangle. I find it easier to pat the dough out by hand rather than use a rolling pin. Cut each rectangle in half horizontally, then into 6 equal pieces vertically, for a total of 24 pieces.

5. Pat a piece of dough between your palms to make a square approximately 3½ inches. Place a heaping tablespoon of filling in the center. Pull up the corners to meet in the center, then pinch and twist to seal. Place on the prepared baking sheet, seam side down. Repeat with the remaining dough and filling.

6. Whisk the egg and water in a small bowl. Baste each knish with egg wash, then sprinkle with the seeds, if using, while still tacky.

7. Bake for 15 to 17 minutes, or until the tops are lightly browned. Allow the knishes to cool for 10 minutes before enjoying.

Cook's Note | Leeks tend to have dirt stuck between the layers, so they need a bit more prep than simply chopping. After cutting them into rounds, pull the layers apart and rinse them in a colander under cold running water.

"Fancy" Beef Crostini

At a fancy party, you'd see this appetizer made with rare beef carpaccio or a sliver of tenderloin, but I find they are just as delicious made with rare roast beef from the deli counter. Just ask for it to be sliced superthin. For an even easier switch-up, you can use crostini from the market, but these little toasts are easy to make from a baguette. Instead of the usual creamy horseradish sauce, I like to mix it up with an extragarlicky aioli. Personalize your tray with a variety of toppings.

PREP TIME | 15 minutes   **COOK TIME** | 20 minutes   **MAKES** | 20 crostini

1 (20-inch) baguette or
  2 (12-inch) baguettes

2 tablespoons extra-virgin
  olive oil

¾ cup Quick Garlic Aioli
  (page 132)

5 slices rare roast beef, cut into
  quarters

1 tablespoon chopped fresh
  chives

OPTIONAL TOPPINGS

  Shaved or crumbled cooked
  egg yolk

  Capers

  Minced red onion

  Grape tomato quarters

  Chopped curly parsley

  Red, pink, or black
  finishing salt

  Drizzle of olive oil

  Black caviar

1 Preheat the oven to 350°F (180°C).

2 Cut the bread into 20 thin slices. Place on a rimmed baking sheet and baste with the oil. Bake for 15 to 20 minutes, or until barely browned and crunchy like croutons. Allow to cool.

3 Evenly slather the crostini with the aioli. Drape a piece of quartered roast beef onto each slice and top with chives, or as desired.

Beef Wellington Tartlets

Traditional beef Wellington is a tenderloin of beef covered in duxelles (mushroom and shallot paste) and usually a layer of bacon or prosciutto, all encased in puff pastry. I am still mastering the challenge, so I developed a recipe that is just as tasty but so easy that my 3-year-old daughter helps me make it.

These tartlets are manageable, and there's a better pastry-meat-duxelles ratio in a smaller serving. The cream cheese adds a rich, homey texture. You can make beef especially for this appetizer or use leftovers. I've substituted New York strip and even sirloin. As long as the cooked beef is tender, the tartlets will be a success.

PREP TIME | 15 minutes   **COOK TIME** | 30 minutes   **MAKES** | 18 tartlets

1 shallot, roughly chopped

1 cup roughly chopped white mushrooms

1 garlic clove, roughly chopped

1 tablespoon unsalted butter

1 teaspoon fresh thyme

1 teaspoon Dijon mustard

2 sheets (1 box) frozen puff pastry, thawed

6 ounces cream cheese, softened

1½ cups cooked beef, cut into 1-inch pieces

1 Preheat the oven to 350°F (180°C). Coat two muffin tins with cooking spray.

2 In a small food processor, combine the shallot, mushrooms, and garlic. Pulse until a coarse paste forms.

3 Heat the butter in a small skillet over medium heat. Add the mushroom paste and cook, stirring frequently, until the mixture is dry and fragrant, approximately 5 minutes. Remove from the heat and stir in the thyme and mustard.

4 Unroll the thawed puff pastry and cut each sheet into nine squares. Press a square into each muffin cup, letting the corners flop over the sides. Equally divide the cream cheese between each cup, about 1 heaping teaspoon. Repeat with the mushroom mixture and then the beef.

5 Bake for 15 to 17 minutes, or until the pastry is puffy and lightly browned on the edges. Serve hot.

> **Cook's Note** | If you like, you can cook filet mignon to use in these tartlets. Before cooking, tie the individual steaks with cooking twine around the "waist" (see page 123). Season with kosher salt and freshly ground pepper, then sear in a skillet over medium-high heat until medium rare (135°F/57°C), approximately 4 minutes on each side. The meat will continue to cook in the oven, so even if you prefer your beef to be well done, it needs to be a little under-cooked to start.
>
> Allow to cool before cutting into smaller pieces. Filet mignon is a tender enough cut that even if you like yours black and blue (nearly raw), a medium cook will still give you butter-smooth bites.

Beefy White Queso

Queso can be served as a stand-alone dip or used as a sauce over burritos, nachos, enchiladas, and more. (Who am I kidding? I eat it with a spoon when no one is watching!) I spent years trying to perfect "restaurant-style" white queso; then one day I simply asked the server at our favorite Mexican joint, and the answer shocked me. The trick is white American cheese (gasp!).

American melts well and creates that perfectly smooth and velvety texture. But the thing that really sets this recipe apart is nutmeg. Most people don't associate nutmeg with cheese dip or even Mexican food, but warm spices such as nutmeg and cinnamon are quite common in Mexican cuisine.

PREP TIME | 10 minutes   COOK TIME | 15 minutes   MAKES | 4 cups

2 tablespoons unsalted butter

½ cup minced white onion

2 garlic cloves, finely minced

1 tablespoon all-purpose flour

¾ cup whole milk

2 cups shredded white American cheese

1 cup shredded pepper Jack cheese

1 teaspoon kosher salt

½ teaspoon ground white pepper

½ teaspoon ground nutmeg

½ cup cooked ground beef

1 Heat the butter in a medium saucepan over medium heat. Add the onion and garlic, sautéing until soft, about 5 minutes.

2 Whisk in the flour until it forms a paste. Then whisk in the milk and heat for 2 to 3 minutes, or until the mixture starts to simmer.

3 Add the cheeses, whisking until melted. Then stir in the salt, pepper, nutmeg, and beef.

4 Serve hot with chips or crudités.

Freezer Friendly: Store in an airtight container for up to 3 months.

Cook's Notes | To make a spicy dip, use a cheese laced with habanero or ghost pepper instead of pepper Jack and add ½ teaspoon red pepper flakes or Aleppo pepper or mince up a fresh jalapeño and toss it in. For a milder version, swap out the pepper Jack for plain Monterey Jack or white American.

   This recipe makes a good amount of dip. Reheat it in a saucepan over low heat, adding 2 to 3 tablespoons of milk and stirring until evenly warmed.

Beefy Blue Cheese & Garlic Mushrooms

Stuffed mushrooms are always a winning appetizer—but forget the typical cream cheese or breadcrumb filling. Instead, stuff them with ground beef and pungent blue cheese, enhanced with an herb butter that bastes the mushrooms from the inside out to impart even more flavor. These appetizers are easy enough to make while watching football in sweats but elegant enough for a dinner party.

PREP TIME | 10 minutes   **COOK TIME** | 15 minutes   **MAKES** | 16 mushroom caps

- 4 tablespoons unsalted butter, softened
- 2 garlic cloves, finely minced
- 2 tablespoons finely minced white onion
- 2 teaspoons finely minced fresh rosemary
- 2 teaspoons finely minced fresh flat-leaf parsley
- 1 tablespoon blue cheese crumbles
- ¼ cup cooked ground beef, drained
- 16 white mushrooms, stems removed
- Maldon sea salt and freshly ground black pepper

1 Preheat the oven to 400°F (200°C). Coat a medium baking dish with cooking spray.

2 Stir together the butter, garlic, onion, rosemary, parsley, and cheese in a small bowl. When fully mixed, fold in the beef.

3 Spoon the filling into the mushroom caps, dividing it as evenly as possible, and place the filled caps into the prepared dish. Bake for 15 to 17 minutes, or until the tops are lightly browned.

4 Sprinkle with salt and pepper, and serve hot.

Cook's Note | Mushrooms are rather fragile and cannot simply be tossed into a colander and rinsed. Instead, pop off the stem and use a damp paper towel to delicately wipe away any surface dirt.

Cheesy Stuffed Jalapeños

These quick, easy, and delicious treats are great to make ahead, then quickly reheat before a party. They also travel well to picnics, potlucks, and tailgates. And you can throw them on the grill if you're cooking outside!

Jalapeños can vary in heat from pepper to pepper, but nearly all will lose some of their potency when seeded and cooked. This recipe allows the heat to be tamed slightly while leaving a little snap. Look for large, cavernous peppers so they have enough space for stuffing.

PREP TIME | 15 minutes   **COOK TIME** | 15 minutes   **MAKES** | 12 pieces

½ cup cooked ground beef

4 ounces cream cheese, softened

¾ cup finely shredded cheddar cheese

¼ teaspoon kosher salt

¼ teaspoon paprika

¼ teaspoon garlic powder

6 large fresh jalapeños, cut in half lengthwise and seeded

1 Preheat the oven to 350°F (180°C). Coat a baking dish with cooking spray.

2 Mash together the beef, cream cheese, ½ cup of the cheddar, and the salt, paprika, and garlic powder in a small bowl.

3 Evenly divide the mixture into the jalapeño halves and place them in the prepared baking dish. Sprinkle with the remaining ¼ cup cheddar. Bake for 15 minutes, or until the cheese melts.

GRILL METHOD

Heat the grill to about 350°F (180°C). Place the jalapeños in an aluminum pan with several holes in the bottom to release liquids. Cook over indirect heat until the cheese melts.

Cook's Notes | Jalapeños release oils that can burn your skin and be very uncomfortable. When working with chiles, wear food-grade (powder-free) gloves. Plastic baggies work in a pinch. Word to the wise: If you do touch them, do not touch your eyes!

A yummy variation is to wrap the jalapeños in parcooked bacon (precooked, but not crispy). Before cooking the peppers, secure the bacon strips with toothpicks soaked in water.

HEFTY
Soups, Stews & Chili

In addition to its classic role in stews and chilis, beef is a wonderful protein choice for piping hot bowls of soup. While many other meats tend to get rubbery when simmered and stewed, the correct cut of beef will end up being melt-in-your-mouth juicy. Embrace your stockpot and bring out some oversize bowls and wide spoons for these beefy delights.

Bacon Cheeseburger in a Bowl

When I first encountered this soup at a friend's holiday party, I was amazed by the flavors and set out to make my own. While researching, I found many recipes with ingredients that I would never put on a burger. Carrots? No. Celery? Not a chance. My version uses only elements you'd find in a bacon cheeseburger, plus fries.

In addition to bacon, cheese, lettuce, onion, and tomato, there's mayo (actually sour cream, because real mayo didn't test well) and a toasted bun (okay, those are the croutons floating on top). Russet potatoes serve as the "fries" and add starchy structure and texture to this burger in a bowl. It's a concoction that would make Jimmy Buffett proud, although I'm not sure you'd want a bowl of soup in paradise.

PREP TIME | 20 minutes   COOK TIME | 20 minutes   SERVES | 6

- 1 tablespoon vegetable oil
- 1 pound 80% lean ground beef
- 2 tablespoons unsalted butter
- ½ cup chopped white onion
- 1 Russet potato, peeled and cut into 1-inch cubes
- ¼ cup all-purpose flour
- 4 cups low-sodium chicken or vegetable broth
- 2 cups whole milk
- 1 teaspoon garlic powder
- ½ teaspoon kosher salt
- ½ teaspoon freshly ground black pepper
- 2 cups shredded cheddar cheese
- ½ cup sour cream
- 2 medium tomatoes, seeded and pulp removed, coarsely chopped
- 1 cup shredded iceberg lettuce
- 1 cup crumbled cooked bacon
- 1 cup garlic croutons

1. Heat the oil in a medium skillet over high heat. Add the beef and brown until no pink remains, about 9 minutes. Crumble into smaller bits. Drain and set aside.

2. Melt the butter in a large Dutch oven or pot over medium heat. Add the onion and potato, and sauté until the onion starts to soften and the potato cubes brown, 3 to 4 minutes. Add the flour, tossing to coat. Stir in the broth, milk, garlic powder, salt, and pepper, and bring to a low simmer. Simmer over low, stirring occasionally, until the potatoes are soft, about 10 minutes.

3. Stir in the cheese and sour cream until both are incorporated and the mixture is slightly thickened. Right before serving, add the beef and the tomatoes, and cook until the tomatoes heat through but not so long that they lose their shape.

4. Top each bowl with lettuce, bacon, croutons, and any other burger-topping favorites.

> **Cook's Note** | Freshly grated cheese is best for smooth melting. Packaged versions are great for quick dinners, but the cheese is commonly tossed in starch to prevent sticking, which can alter the texture of the soup.

Smoky Steak Chili

Steak chili is a combination of soup, stew, and traditional chili. I tasted this particular recipe years ago at a chili cook-off, where it took the blue ribbon. I've modified it several times, keeping the basics that make it so delicious.

Instead of ground beef, this recipe calls for bottom round cut into chunks, browned, and simmered in dark beer to give it a distinctly different flavor from the sauce, which is puréed instead of left coarse. I highly recommend serving this chili over a bed of rice or pasta to soak up the extra sauce.

PREP TIME | 40 minutes   **COOK TIME** | 2 hours 45 minutes   **SERVES** | 12

3–4 pounds bottom round roast, trimmed and cut into 1–2-inch pieces

1 teaspoon kosher salt

1 teaspoon freshly ground black pepper

1 tablespoon ground cumin

2 tablespoons plus 2 teaspoons vegetable oil

12 ounces dark beer, such as a porter or stout

2 cups chopped red onion

1 poblano chile, seeded and chopped

1 jalapeño, seeded and chopped

6 garlic cloves

4 chipotle chiles in adobo sauce

1 (24-ounce) can crushed tomatoes

1 (14.5-ounce) can petite diced tomatoes

1 (8-ounce) can tomato paste

1 tablespoon ancho chile powder

2 cups low-sodium beef broth

3 tablespoons honey

1. Arrange an oven rack in the lower-third position and preheat the oven to 300°F (150°C).

2. Toss the beef with the salt, black pepper, and cumin in a large bowl.

3. Heat 2 tablespoons of the oil in a large Dutch oven or ovenproof stockpot over medium heat. Working in three batches, add the cubed meat, tossing to brown the exterior. Transfer the browned meat to a paper towel–lined plate and repeat with the other batches.

4. When all the meat is browned, deglaze the pot with the beer, scraping up the browned bits from the bottom. Return the beef to the pot and reduce the heat to low. Simmer, uncovered, for 10 to 15 minutes, or until most of the liquid has evaporated.

5. Meanwhile, in a separate skillet, heat the remaining 2 teaspoons oil over medium heat. Add the onion, poblano, and jalapeño. Cook for about 5 minutes, or until the onion is soft and opaque. Stir in the garlic and cook for 2 to 3 minutes longer.

6. Using a slotted spoon, transfer the beef pieces from the pot to a bowl. Stir the cooked onion mixture into the beer. Add the chipotles, crushed tomatoes, diced tomatoes, tomato paste, and ancho chile powder. Stir together and then, using an immersion blender, blend until fairly smooth. The mixture will still have texture and body, but not large pieces. If you don't own an immersion blender, transfer the mixture to a food processor or leave as a chunky chili.

7. Stir in the beef broth and return the cooked beef. Cover and braise in the oven for 2 hours. Stir in the honey just before serving.

Freezer Friendly: Freeze in an airtight container for up to 3 months. Allow to fully thaw before reheating over medium heat.

Cook's Note | One tip I've taken to heart is never to serve a bowl of soup without adorning it with at least three toppings. For any bowl of chili, I recommend something crunchy to liven up the texture, something smooth to add body, and something cool to soothe the spiciness.

- Diced avocado
- Shredded cheese
- Sour cream
- Salty crackers
- Shredded iceberg lettuce
- Scallions or chives
- Pepitas
- Fresh cilantro or parsley
- Diced red onion

Italian Meatball Soup

Hearty, easy-to-make meatball soup is a staple in many Italian households. Every good nonna (Italian grandma) has a stash of homemade meatballs in the freezer. No one needs to know if you cut a few corners and throw in your favorite store-bought variety—the simple, flavorful broth will make them feel right at home.

Orzo is a nice small pasta, the ideal spoon size, but feel free to use any pasta shape you prefer. Vermicelli, ditalini, and fusilli are great choices, too. I like to top this soup with freshly grated Parmesan cheese, a sprinkle of Maldon salt, and a few buttery croutons.

PREP TIME | 30 minutes   COOK TIME | 1 hour   SERVES | 4

FOR THE MEATBALLS

- 1 pound 80% lean ground beef
- 1 egg, lightly beaten
- ¼ cup seasoned breadcrumbs
- ¼ cup finely minced white onion
- 1 garlic clove, finely minced
- 1 teaspoon Worcestershire sauce
- ¼ teaspoon kosher salt
- ¼ teaspoon freshly ground black pepper

FOR THE SOUP

- 2 tablespoons extra-virgin olive oil
- 1 cup chopped white onion
- 1 cup thinly sliced carrots
- 3 garlic cloves, minced
- 6 cups low-sodium chicken broth
- 1 (14-ounce) can petite diced tomatoes
- 1 tablespoon minced fresh oregano
- 1 tablespoon minced fresh flat-leaf parsley
- 1 teaspoon minced fresh basil
- 1 cup uncooked orzo pasta
- 2 tablespoons finely grated Parmesan cheese, plus more for topping
- 1 tablespoon red wine vinegar
  Butter croutons
  Maldon sea salt and freshly ground black pepper

1 **Make the meatballs:** Preheat the oven to 400°F (200°C). Coat a 9- by 13-inch baking dish with cooking spray.

2 Mix the beef with the egg, breadcrumbs, onion, garlic, Worcestershire, salt, and pepper until thoroughly combined. Roll into 1½-inch meatballs, placing them in the prepared baking dish. Bake for 15 minutes, then use a slotted spoon to transfer the meatballs to a paper towel–lined plate.

3 **Make the soup:** Meanwhile, heat the oil in a large Dutch oven or pot over medium heat. Sauté the onion, carrots, and garlic for 4 to 5 minutes, or until fragrant and starting to soften. Add the broth, tomatoes, oregano, parsley, and basil, stirring well. Reduce heat to low and bring the soup to a low simmer. Add the pasta and meatballs, and simmer until the pasta is cooked al dente, 10 to 12 minutes.

4 Stir in the 2 tablespoons Parmesan until melted and smooth. Add the vinegar and serve the soup immediately, topping each bowl with additional Parmesan, some croutons, and a sprinkling of salt and pepper.

Cook's Note | I prefer fresh herbs for this simple base, but dried is fine, if that's what you have on hand. Because dried herbs have more concentrated flavor, substitute 1 teaspoon dried for every 1 tablespoon fresh. Rubbing them between your palms before adding them to the recipe will release natural oils and enhance flavor.

Red Wine Beef Stew

There's nothing quite like a steaming bowl of beef stew on a chilly winter night. It's like your food is giving you a giant hug. What makes this recipe extraspecial is that instead of requiring a long simmering time to tenderize the meat, it calls for a New York strip steak, because that's what I had on hand when I first created this stew. That was years ago, but I still prefer the same cut because it results in the tastiest, melt-in-your-mouth beef stew you've ever eaten while also reducing the cook time to less than an hour. Red wine and hearty root vegetables add sophistication to the cooked-all-day flavor. What's not to warm your heart?

PREP TIME | 25 minutes   COOK TIME | 50 minutes   SERVES | 6

3 tablespoons all-purpose flour

2 teaspoons coarse sea salt

1 teaspoon paprika
   Freshly ground black pepper

2 pounds New York strip (2 large steaks), trimmed, cut into 1-inch pieces, and patted dry

2 tablespoons extra-virgin olive oil

1½ cups dry red wine

4 cups low-sodium beef broth

½ teaspoon ground thyme

2 bay leaves

½ cup chopped white onion

6 ounces rutabaga, peeled and cut into 1-inch cubes, about ¾ cup

¾ cup julienned carrots

¾ cup julienned parsnips

½ pound small red potatoes, quartered

1 cup sliced cremini mushrooms
   Fresh oregano leaves and grated Parmesan cheese, for topping
   Loaf of crusty bread, for serving

1. Combine the flour, 1 teaspoon of the salt, the paprika, and ½ teaspoon pepper in a medium bowl. Set aside 2 tablespoons of the mixture to thicken the stew at the end. Toss the beef with the remaining flour mixture, shaking off the excess flour.

2. Heat the oil in a large Dutch oven or pot over medium-high heat. Working in batches, sear the beef, turning the cubes every so often to brown the outside. The meat does not have to be fully cooked. Cook each batch for 4 to 5 minutes, then transfer to a paper towel–lined plate.

3. Deglaze the pot with the wine, scraping the bottom to incorporate all those little browned bits that will dissolve and add flavor. Stir in the broth, thyme, and bay leaves. Reduce heat to medium and bring the liquid to a low simmer before returning the cooked beef to the pot.

4. Add the onion, rutabaga, carrots, parsnips, potatoes, and mushrooms, and bring back to a simmer over medium heat. Cook for 15 to 18 minutes, or until the vegetables are soft when pierced with a fork.

5. Ladle ¼ cup of the broth into a small bowl and whisk in the reserved 2 tablespoons flour mixture until smooth. Add this paste to the stew. Cook for 5 minutes longer. The cooking liquid should coat the back of a spoon, but not be thick like gravy. Add the remaining 1 teaspoon salt, and season to taste with additional pepper.

6. Ladle into bowls, top with fresh oregano and Parmesan, and serve with slices of crusty bread to soak up every drop.

Freezer Friendly: Freeze an extra batch or single servings in airtight containers for up to 3 months. Thin with water or beef broth if it's too thick when thawed.

Vietnamese-Inspired Beef & Rice Noodles

It takes hours to make a perfect pho, that Vietnamese masterpiece of complex flavors in a smooth broth, gently braised with fresh, crispy veggies on top, and maybe even a jammy soft-cooked egg.

This recipe mimics those flavors in a fraction of the time. Instead of roasting bones to make broth from scratch, you infuse a beef broth with the warm spices of anise and cinnamon, piquant peppercorns, and fresh ginger to create a flavorful base for pan-seared sirloin, the best option for tender beef in a jiffy.

Top with your favorite pho toppings such as scallions, fresh Thai basil, jalapeños, bean sprouts, and a spritz of lime juice to brighten everything up.

PREP TIME | 15 minutes   **COOK TIME** | 40 minutes   **SERVES** | 4

1 pound rice noodles	
1–2 teaspoons sesame oil	
10–12 cups low-sodium beef broth	
	1-inch piece fresh ginger, peeled and cut into strips
3	garlic cloves, lightly smashed
¼	white onion
1	tablespoon whole black peppercorns
1	tablespoon fish sauce
1	cinnamon stick
2	star anise pods
1½	pounds top sirloin
½	teaspoon coarse kosher salt
¼	teaspoon freshly ground black pepper
	Fresh lime wedges

OPTIONAL TOPPINGS

Thai basil leaves
Sriracha sauce
Fresh jalapeño slices
Soft-boiled egg
Bean sprouts
Hoisin sauce

1 Cook the noodles according to package directions. Rinse with cold water to stop the cooking, then toss with the oil, using just enough to prevent the noodles from sticking. Set aside.

2 Combine the broth, ginger, garlic, onion, peppercorns, fish sauce, cinnamon stick, and star anise pods in a medium saucepan over medium heat. Bring to a low simmer. Simmer for 30 minutes, then pour the liquid through a colander or fine-mesh sieve. Discard the solids and keep the broth warm until ready to serve.

3 While the broth simmers, season both sides of the beef with the salt and pepper. Heat a large skillet over medium-high heat, then sear the meat for 2 to 3 minutes on each side, until cooked to medium doneness (145°F/63°C). Transfer to a cutting board and let rest for 5 minutes.

4 Slice the beef thinly against the grain. Ladle the broth into large soup bowls and evenly divide the sliced beef among the bowls. Serve with a lime wedge and your favorite toppings.

Beefy Tomato & Macaroni Soup

This kid-friendly classic is best served with a gooey grilled cheese sandwich. To make it more appealing to tiny taste buds, I swapped out chopped garlic and onion for their powdered counterparts to give a little flavor without those offensive pieces. You can take it one step further and purée the broth, although I like leaving chunks of tomato.

That said, this version is adult friendly, with a dab of cream for texture and a splash of balsamic vinegar for a zingy and sweet aftertaste. You can easily customize this soup by adding more or less tomato, broth, beef, or pasta.

PREP TIME | 5 minutes   COOK TIME | 25 minutes   SERVES | 6

1 tablespoon vegetable oil

1 pound 80% lean ground beef

4 cups low-sodium beef broth

1 (14.5-ounce) can petite diced tomatoes

1 (15-ounce) can plain tomato sauce

2 teaspoons onion powder

2 teaspoons garlic powder

1 teaspoon Italian seasoning

1 tablespoon Worcestershire sauce

1 tablespoon balsamic vinegar

1 cup dry ditalini or other small alphabet or ring-shaped pasta

2 tablespoons heavy cream

Shredded Parmesan or cheddar cheese and garlic croutons, for garnish

1 Heat the oil in a large pot or Dutch oven over high heat. Add the beef, browning and breaking it apart as it cooks, 8 to 10 minutes. Drain and return to the pot.

2 Stir in the broth, diced tomatoes, tomato sauce, onion powder, garlic powder, Italian seasoning, Worcestershire, and vinegar. Reduce heat to medium and bring the mixture to a low simmer. Add the pasta and cook for 8 minutes, or until the pasta is al dente.

3 Stir in the cream and garnish with shredded cheese and garlic croutons.

Freezer Friendly: Pasta doesn't freeze well, so if you make a batch of this soup to freeze for future meals, leave it out. Add cooked pasta after thawing and reheating the soup. Freeze in an airtight container for up to 3 months.

Winter Beef & Barley Soup

Making a standout soup is all about creating layered flavors. Three things make this soup different from a standard beef-and-veggies-in-broth version. The first is browning the meat to develop a robust, savory flavor and roasting the root vegetables so they keep their toothy texture and individual taste. The second trick is incorporating parsnip, which in my view is one of the most underused root vegetables. Its creamy sweetness adds depth and texture. Third, add a tablespoon of acid right before serving. No soup is complete until it has been splashed with citrus juice, vinegar, or wine.

PREP TIME | 15 minutes   COOK TIME | 1 hour   SERVES | 8

- 2 tablespoons extra-virgin olive oil
- 2 teaspoons kosher salt
- 2 teaspoons freshly ground black pepper
- 1 large russet potato, peeled and cut into 1-inch pieces
- 2 medium carrots, peeled and cut into bite-size slices
- 1 large parsnip, peeled and cut into bite-size slices
- 2 tablespoons all-purpose flour
- 2 pounds chuck roast, trimmed and cut into 2-inch pieces
- ½ cup chopped white onion
- 2 garlic cloves, minced
- 6 cups low-sodium beef broth
- 1 (14.5-ounce) can petite diced tomatoes
- ⅔ cup medium-grain dry barley
- 1 tablespoon dry beef bouillon powder
- 1 tablespoon Worcestershire sauce
- 1 tablespoon dried parsley flakes
- 1 bay leaf
- 1 tablespoon red wine vinegar
- Sour cream, celery leaves, and garlic croutons, for topping (optional)

1. Preheat the oven to 400°F (200°C). Line a rimmed baking sheet with aluminum foil.

2. Combine 1 tablespoon of the oil, 1 teaspoon of the salt, and 1 teaspoon of the pepper with the potato, carrots, and parsnip in a medium bowl. Toss well. Transfer the veggies to the prepared baking sheet, shaking off the excess oil. Roast for 25 minutes, or until browned and soft when pierced with a fork. Set aside to cool.

3. Meanwhile, combine the flour, remaining 1 teaspoon salt, and remaining 1 teaspoon pepper in a separate medium bowl. Toss with the beef until coated.

4. Heat the remaining 1 tablespoon oil in a large Dutch oven or pot (minimum of 7½ quarts) over medium heat. Shake off the excess flour and add the beef to the hot oil. Cook until brown on all sides, about 5 minutes.

5. Add the onion and garlic to the pot and cook for 1 to 2 minutes longer, until the onion starts to soften. Stir in the broth, tomatoes, barley, bouillon, Worcestershire, parsley, and bay leaf, and bring to a low simmer over medium heat. Simmer, uncovered, for 40 minutes, stirring occasionally.

6. Just before serving, stir in the roasted vegetables and vinegar. Top with sour cream, celery leaves, and croutons, if desired.

Freezer Friendly: Barley freezes and thaws better in soups than pasta. Make an extra batch for later, or freeze in single-serving containers for an easy meal on the go. Keeps for up to 3 months.

Continued on next page

Winter Beef & Barley Soup, *continued*

Cook's Notes | Many cuts of beef are acceptable for soups and stews, but for one that has a long simmer time, a chuck roast, chuck shoulder, chuck-eye roast, or top chuck are top picks. Cutting the roast into smaller pieces reduces the amount of time needed to transform the meat into tender morsels.

Note that barley will absorb liquid after cooking, so the soup may thicken when cooled. Add more broth or water to thin it to the desired consistency when reheating.

If your family doesn't care for barley, you can substitute cooked pasta or rice, added right before serving. Don't add it too early or it will get soggy and bloated.

I usually top this dish with sour cream, celery leaves, and garlic croutons, but it is perfect with no toppings at all.

4

BEEFY-LICIOUS
Salads

The addition of beef elevates a mere bowl of mixed greens and chopped veggies. These hearty salads work as entrées and are guaranteed to leave you feeling satisfied. When I tell you these salads are craveable, I'm not kidding. Juicy slices of steak, tender ground beef, and savory morsels combined with varied colors and textures make them a winning choice any time.

And of course, the salad dressing is key. My advice is make your own—it doesn't take long, you can experiment with different flavors, and when you find one you like, you can whip up a big batch.

Southwest Steak Salad with Chipotle Ranch Dressing

I've come to love a large, luscious salad as a meal, but I know that for some people, even a big salad isn't enough to fill them up. This hearty dish is built around tender, flavorful steak; is packed with colorful veggies; and boasts a spicy dressing that can be modified to suit your taste buds. Chips and guacamole are the perfect sides to pair with this zesty salad.

PREP TIME | 20 minutes active; 4 hours to marinate
COOK TIME | 8 minutes   **SERVES** | 4 as entrée

FOR THE STEAK

- ½ cup water
- ¼ cup vegetable oil, plus 1 tablespoon for greasing
- 1 garlic clove, minced
- 1 teaspoon kosher salt
- ½ teaspoon freshly ground black pepper
- ½ teaspoon chili powder
- 1 tablespoon fresh cilantro leaves, rubbed between your palms
- Zest and juice from 1 lime
- 1½ pounds flat iron steak

FOR THE SALAD

- 8 cups fresh baby spinach
- 1 cup chopped red bell pepper
- ¼ cup roughly chopped fresh cilantro leaves
- 1 (15-ounce) can black beans, rinsed and drained
- 1 (15-ounce) can corn, rinsed and drained
- 1 cup halved grape tomatoes
- Chipotle Ranch Dressing (recipe follows)
- Handful of tortilla chips, lightly crushed

1 **Make the steak:** Combine the water, ¼ cup oil, garlic, salt, black pepper, chili powder, cilantro, and lime zest and juice in a shallow dish or airtight plastic bag. Whisk or massage until blended. Add the steak and marinate in the refrigerator for at least 4 hours, preferably overnight.

2 To cook, heat a large cast-iron pan over medium-high heat. If the pan is not well seasoned, lightly grease it with the 1 tablespoon oil. Sear the steak on one side for 2 to 3 minutes, pressing down to make sure the entire piece makes contact with the hot pan. Flip and sear the other side. The meat should be cooked to medium rare (135°F/57°C) at this point. Cook longer if the steak is thicker than 1 inch or if you want the meat more well done.

3 Transfer the steak to a cutting board and allow to rest for 5 minutes. Cut the meat against the grain into slender strips or chop into bite-size cubes.

4 **Assemble the salad:** Divide the spinach, bell pepper, cilantro, beans, corn, and tomatoes among four large salad bowls. Top each with a portion of the steak, drizzle with the ranch dressing, and garnish with crushed tortilla chips.

> Cook's Note | Long, thin slices look so pretty on salads, but managing a steak knife in a bowl can be tricky. Do yourself a favor and chop the steak into bite-size pieces before plating. You'll still have a dazzling salad; it will just be more fork friendly.

Chipotle Ranch Dressing

> Makes 1 cup

- ½ cup mayonnaise
- ½ cup milk
- 1 tablespoon dry ranch seasoning
- 1 chipotle chile in adobo sauce
- 1 teaspoon lime zest
- 1 teaspoon lime juice

Combine the mayonnaise, milk, ranch seasoning, chipotle, lime zest, and lime juice in a food processor until fully mixed. You can make the dressing mild by omitting the chipotle; alternatively, amp up the spice by doubling the chile amount. Store in an airtight container in the refrigerator for up to 1 week.

Easy, Everyday Guac

If you don't have a favorite guacamole recipe, this quick version is perfect with this salad.

> Makes 1½ cups

- 2 ripe avocados, cut into chunks
- ¼ cup sour cream
- ½ teaspoon coarse sea salt
- 1 garlic clove, finely minced
- 2 teaspoons lime juice

Combine the avocados, sour cream, salt, garlic, and lime juice in a medium bowl and mash with a fork until blended.

Taco Salad with Ranchero Sauce

I like a taco salad to be literally a deconstructed taco—and because I don't put salad dressing on a taco, I opt for homemade ranchero sauce. It has a little bit more body than straight-up hot sauce but is still loose enough to be taco-worthy. To really hit the taco theme, serve this salad in a tostada bowl.

PREP TIME | 20 minutes   COOK TIME | 35 minutes   SERVES | 4 as entrée

- 2 teaspoons vegetable oil
- 1 pound 90% lean ground beef
- 1 packet taco seasoning
- ½ cup low-sodium beef broth
- ½ cup chunky salsa (mild, medium, or hot, as desired)
- 1 teaspoon ground cumin
- 1 cup sour cream
- 1 head iceberg lettuce, shredded
- 1 cup diced fresh tomatoes
- 1 cup shredded or cubed pepper Jack cheese
- 1 avocado, cut into chunks
- 1 cup tortilla chips, slightly crumbled
  Ranchero Sauce (recipe follows)

Cook's Note | Homemade ranchero takes about 15 minutes to prepare, but you can always use your favorite store or restaurant brand. Making it at home gives you the advantage of controlling the heat by adding more or less fresh jalapeño and chile powder.

1 Heat the oil in a large skillet over high heat. Add the beef, breaking it apart as it cooks. Drain off any fat and return the meat to the skillet. (With very lean meat, you may not need to drain it.)

2 Stir the taco seasoning and broth into the meat, then simmer over low heat for 5 minutes. Add the salsa, stirring to combine.

3 Stir the cumin into the sour cream in a small bowl.

4 Divide the lettuce, tomatoes, cheese, avocado, and tortilla chips among four large salad bowls or plates. Top each serving with some taco meat, a dollop of the sour cream mixture, and a tablespoon of ranchero sauce (a little goes a long way).

Ranchero Sauce

Makes 1 cup

- 1 tablespoon extra-virgin olive oil
- ½ cup chopped white onion
- 1 fresh jalapeño, seeded and minced
- 1 garlic clove, minced
- 1½ cups plain tomato sauce
- ½ cup low-sodium chicken broth
- 2 tablespoons lime juice
- 1 teaspoon dried oregano
- ½ teaspoon kosher salt
- ½ teaspoon smoked paprika
- ½ teaspoon chili powder

1 Heat the oil in a medium saucepan over medium heat. Add the onion, jalapeño, and garlic, and cook until soft and fragrant, about 5 minutes.

2 Add the tomato sauce, broth, lime juice, oregano, salt, paprika, and chili powder, stirring to combine. Reduce the heat to low and simmer for 5 minutes.

3 Remove the pan from the heat. Let the mixture cool, then blend until smooth by using an immersion blender or transferring the mixture to a stand blender or food processor.

4 Use the sauce on tacos, as a dip, or spooned over eggs. Leftover sauce can be stored for up to a week in the refrigerator.

Spinach, Apple & Fennel Salad

with Warm Bacon & Shallot Dressing

This is one of my favorite salads, although I feel like that about *all* of these salads. It is hearty and green with unexpected opposing flavors of bitter and sweet. If I am making it for visitors or a special occasion, I pull out my mandoline slicer for paper-thin cuts of fragrant fennel and tart apple. But for a casual weeknight meal, I just chop everything coarsely.

PREP TIME | 10 minutes   **COOK TIME** | 15 minutes   **SERVES** | 4 as entrée

- 2 (8-ounce) New York strip steaks
- Kosher salt and freshly ground black pepper
- 1–2 teaspoons vegetable oil (optional; see step 2)
- 8 cups fresh baby spinach
- 4 ounces soft goat cheese
- 4 tablespoons coarsely chopped walnuts
- 1 fennel bulb, trimmed and thinly sliced
- 1 tart apple, cored and thinly sliced
- Warm Bacon & Shallot Dressing (recipe follows)

Cook's Note | If you're not familiar with fennel, it's often described as tasting like anise or licorice—but honestly, I don't care for licorice, and I love fennel. It has a fresh crunch and provides a delicate, mild flavor like nothing else.

1. Season both sides of the steaks liberally with salt and pepper.

2. Heat a well-seasoned cast-iron or other nonstick pan over high heat. If using a regular pan, add the oil. When the pan is hot, add the steaks. Sear the steaks on each side for 4 to 5 minutes, pressing down to make sure all the meat makes contact with the hot pan. The meat should be cooked to medium done-ness (145°F/63°C). Transfer the steaks to a cutting board and let rest for 5 minutes.

3. Meanwhile, assemble the salad by evenly dividing the spinach, cheese, walnuts, fennel, and apple among four large salad bowls or plates.

4. Once the steak has rested, cut it into thin slices, discarding any large pieces of fat and evenly dividing the meat among the plates. Spoon some of the warm dressing over each salad and serve.

Warm Bacon & Shallot Dressing

Makes ¾ cup

- 2 teaspoons extra-virgin olive oil
- ¼ cup chopped shallots
- ¼ cup apple cider vinegar
- 2 tablespoons maple syrup
- 1 teaspoon Dijon mustard
- ½ teaspoon kosher salt
- ¼ teaspoon freshly ground black pepper
- ½ cup cooked and chopped bacon

1. Heat the oil in a small saucepan over medium heat. Add the shallots, sautéing until slightly soft. Whisk in the vinegar, maple syrup, mustard, salt, and pepper until combined. Heat for 4 to 5 minutes, or until small bubbles form. Add the bacon, heating for 3 to 4 minutes longer, until the bacon is warmed.

2. The dressing can be made ahead of time and can be refrigerated for up to 4 days. It is best served warm. Reheat it on the stovetop or microwave it on high for 10 to 20 seconds. Stir well before spooning.

Chopped Beef Salad with Spicy Peanut Sauce

This salad came about when I was wondering what to do with leftover beef skewers and satay sauce. Tender meat perfectly seasoned along with a slightly spicy peanut sauce sounded delightful in a salad.

Satay refers to the peanut sauce, not the skewers themselves. Most satay sauces are blended with dry-roasted peanuts, but to save time and not require a heavy-duty blender, I used creamy peanut butter. I like the added crunch of more peanuts, while my husband opts for fried Chinese noodles. Pick your favorite or use both, but don't skip the crunchies!

PREP TIME | 20 minutes active; 3–4 hours to marinate

COOK TIME | 10 minutes   **SERVES** | 4 as entrée

FOR THE BEEF

- ½ cup chopped white onion
- ⅓ cup light soy sauce
- ¼ cup chopped fresh lemongrass
- ¼ cup firmly packed light brown sugar
- 3 garlic cloves, minced
- 3 tablespoons vegetable oil
- 2 tablespoons fish sauce
- 1 tablespoon grated fresh ginger
- 1 tablespoon ground coriander
- 1 teaspoon turmeric powder
- 1 teaspoon ground cumin
- ¼ teaspoon cayenne pepper
- 1 pound Milanese-style beef, cut lengthwise into 1-inch-wide strips (see Cook's Notes)

FOR THE SALAD

- 4 cups thinly sliced or chopped red cabbage
- 4 cups thinly sliced or chopped green cabbage
- 1 cup red bell pepper, seeded and chopped
- 1 cup chopped carrots
- ½ cup chopped scallions
- ½ cup fresh cilantro leaves
- ½ cup dry-roasted peanuts or fried Chinese noodles
  Spicy Peanut Sauce (recipe follows)

1 Make the beef:
Whisk together the onion, soy sauce, lemongrass, sugar, garlic, oil, fish sauce, ginger, coriander, turmeric, cumin, and cayenne in a large bowl until a paste forms. Slather this marinade on the beef and place it in either an airtight plastic bag or a shallow dish. Toss to coat. Cover and refrigerate for 3 to 24 hours.

2 To cook, heat a large nonstick skillet over medium-high heat. Remove the beef from marinade, gently shaking off the excess. Working in batches, add the beef to the hot skillet. Cook for only 1 to 2 minutes, or until lightly browned, then flip the meat and cook on the other side. Transfer to a cutting board and chop into bite-size pieces.

3 Assemble the salad:
Equally divide the red and green cabbages, bell pepper, carrots, and scallions among four large salad bowls or plates. Top each serving with some chopped beef, cilantro, peanuts, and a liberal amount of sauce.

Cook's Notes | Adjust the spiciness of the sauce by adding 1 to 2 more teaspoons of Thai chile garlic sauce, red pepper flakes, Sriracha, or even chopped fresh jalapeño.

If you can find thinly sliced Milanese-style beef at the grocery store, save yourself time and trouble and buy it! If not, partially freeze a top round roast. Beef is easier to thinly slice when a little hard. Using a very sharp knife, cut it into ⅛-inch-thick slices. You might need to cut them in half again vertically to get them 2 inches wide.

Fresh ginger is also easier to grate when slightly frozen.

Continued on next page

Spicy Peanut Sauce

Makes 1½ cups

- ½ cup creamy peanut butter
- ½ cup light coconut milk
- 2 tablespoons light soy sauce
- 1 tablespoon firmly packed light brown sugar
- 1 tablespoon fish sauce
- 1 tablespoon water
- 1–3 teaspoons Thai chile garlic sauce
- ½ teaspoon lime zest
  Juice from 1 lime (1–2 tablespoons)
- 1 garlic clove, grated

1 Whisk the peanut butter, coconut milk, soy sauce, sugar, fish sauce, water, chile garlic sauce, lime zest, and lime juice in a small bowl or blend in a small food processor until well combined.

2 Serve at room temperature or chill until ready to serve. If the sauce thickens, add additional coconut milk or water to thin. The sauce can be refrigerated in an airtight container for up to 1 week.

Steakhouse Salad with Homemade Blue Cheese Dressing

Flank steak is ideal for cutting into beautiful, substantial slices to top a salad. Due to its leanness, it requires the right marinade to tenderize and impart flavor. This marinade teams acidic citrus, salty soy, and sweet brown sugar for a perfect flavor balance that also creates a delicious caramelized crust on the meat.

PREP TIME | 20 minutes active; 12–24 hours to marinate
COOK TIME | 15 minutes   **SERVES** | 4 as entrée

FOR THE STEAK

- ½ cup water
- ⅓ cup vegetable oil
- ⅓ cup low-sodium soy sauce
- 2 tablespoons lemon juice
- 2 tablespoons firmly packed light brown sugar
- 1 teaspoon hot sauce
- 1 teaspoon kosher salt
- 1½ pounds flank steak

FOR THE SALAD

- 8 cups spring salad mix
- ¼ cup halved grape tomatoes
- ¼ cup chopped carrots
- 2 tablespoons diced red onion
- ¼ cup blue cheese crumbles
  Homemade Blue Cheese Dressing (recipe follows)
  Freshly ground black pepper

Cook's Notes | Long, thin steak slices look attractive on a salad but can be tricky to manage, so I suggest cutting the meat into bite-size pieces before plating. You'll still have a delicious salad; it will just be easier to eat!

For an extra kick of flavor, add a drizzle of Balsamic Glaze (page 134) to the Homemade Blue Cheese Dressing.

1 Make the steak: Combine the water, oil, soy sauce, lemon juice, sugar, hot sauce, and salt in an airtight plastic bag or shallow dish. Add the flank steak and marinate in the refrigerator for at least 12, and up to 24, hours, flipping at least once during the marinating time.

2 To grill: Preheat the grill to medium heat (about 350°F/180°C) and oil the grates. Place the steak over direct heat and cook for 5 to 6 minutes on each side. Rest for 5 minutes before slicing against the grain.

To broil: Arrange an oven rack 3 to 4 inches from the heating element and preheat the broiler on high. Line a rimmed baking sheet with aluminum foil, then place the steak on it. Broil for 5 to 6 minutes on each side for medium rare (135°F/57°C). Rest for 5 minutes before slicing against the grain.

3 Assemble the salad: Divide the lettuce, tomatoes, carrots, onion, and cheese among four large bowls or plates. Top with the sliced steak and pour on the blue cheese dressing. Season with pepper.

Homemade Blue Cheese Dressing

Makes 1 cup

- ½ cup mayonnaise
- ¼ cup blue cheese crumbles
- ¼ cup milk
- ¼ cup water
- 2 tablespoons sour cream
- 1 tablespoon lemon juice
- ¼ teaspoon Worcestershire sauce
- ¼ teaspoon kosher salt

Whisk together the mayonnaise, blue cheese, milk, water, sour cream, lemon juice, Worcestershire, and salt in a small bowl. The dressing can be made in advance and stored in the refrigerator, where it will last up to a week.

Lemony Brussels Sprout Salad

Not all salads start with lettuce or traditional leafy greens. Here the base is composed of crispy roasted Brussels sprouts, red potatoes, and onions. Topped with thinly sliced skirt steak and a tangy lemon-herb vinaigrette, it can be served as a small starter or an entire entrée.

PREP TIME | 15 minutes   **COOK TIME** | 40 minutes   **SERVES** | 4 as entrée

- 1 pound Brussels sprouts, trimmed and halved
- 2 large red potatoes, cut into 2-inch cubes
- ½ white onion, thinly sliced
- 1 tablespoon extra-virgin olive oil
- 1 pound skirt steak
  Kosher salt and freshly ground black pepper
- 3–4 tablespoons freshly grated Parmesan cheese
  Lemon Vinaigrette (recipe follows)

1 Preheat the oven to 400°F (200°C). Line a rimmed baking sheet with aluminum foil.

2 Toss together the Brussels sprouts, potatoes, onion, and oil in a medium bowl. Scrape the mixture onto the prepared baking sheet. Roast for 30 minutes, turning once halfway through cooking.

3 Halfway through the vegetable cooking time, heat a large cast-iron pan or nonstick skillet over high heat. Season the steak with salt and pepper on both sides, then drop the steak in the pan, searing for 2 to 3 minutes on each side until just browned. Transfer to a cutting board and let rest for 3 to 4 minutes. Slice into small strips.

4 To assemble the salad, divide the roasted vegetables and the steak evenly among serving dishes. Top each dish with some Parmesan and 1 tablespoon lemon vinaigrette.

Lemon Vinaigrette

Makes ¾ cup

- 1 garlic clove, minced
- 2 teaspoons fresh rosemary
- 2 teaspoons fresh sage
- 2 teaspoons fresh thyme
- 1 teaspoon lemon zest
- 2 tablespoons lemon juice
- ½ teaspoon kosher salt
- ½ teaspoon freshly ground black pepper
- 1 teaspoon Dijon mustard
- 1 teaspoon sugar
- 1 tablespoon red wine vinegar
- ½ cup extra-virgin olive oil

1 Combine the garlic, rosemary, sage, thyme, lemon zest, and lemon juice in a small food processor until mixed well. (Alternatively, finely mince the rosemary, sage, and thyme, then combine with the garlic, lemon zest, and lemon juice in a small bowl.)

2 Add the salt, pepper, mustard, sugar, and vinegar, and mix to create a paste. Whisk in the oil until emulsified.

3 Set the vinaigrette aside for 20 to 30 minutes to allow the flavors to develop. Store leftovers in the refrigerator for up to a week, and shake or stir well before serving.

5

MEATY
Mains

Here we come to the "meat of the book" (pun intended). Beef is usually associated with entrées, and rightfully so with classics like beef stroganoff, steak fajitas, pot roast, and brisket. I enjoyed freshening up some old favorites by sneaking in more veggies, adding a dash of color, or developing time-saving hacks. But you'll also discover other recipes that are sure to become favorites, like Thai Coconut Beef, Super Stuffed Peppers, and Creamy 40-Clove Garlic Beef. Earmark this chapter, because I can guarantee you'll be coming back.

Easy Shredded Beef

For recipes that call for precooked beef, you can generally use leftovers from a pot roast or a strip steak, but sometimes you need to cook the beef first. In that case, I swear by my electric pressure cooker, although a slow cooker will work just fine if you have the time. Make this shredded beef for sandwiches and quesadillas or to top a salad.

PREP TIME | 10 minutes **COOK TIME** | 45 minutes **SERVES** | 5–6

1½ pounds chuck roast

Kosher salt and freshly ground black pepper

1 tablespoon vegetable oil

1½ cups low-sodium beef broth

½ white onion, sliced

3 garlic cloves, lightly mashed

2 bay leaves

STOVETOP METHOD

Cut the roast into four or five pieces. Season each with salt and pepper. Heat the oil in a large skillet over medium-high heat. Brown the meat well on both sides. Add the broth, onion, garlic, and bay leaves, and reduce to low heat. Cover and braise for 2 hours, turning once halfway through. Remove the meat from the skillet, draining off any liquid. Let the meat cool slightly, then shred using two forks, discarding any large fatty pieces.

PRESSURE COOKER METHOD

Heat the oil using the sauté function. Season the beef with salt and pepper, and sear it until browned on all sides. Add the broth, onion, garlic, and bay leaves to the pot. Seal and cook on manual high pressure for 30 minutes. Release the pressure using the quick release function. Remove the meat from the pot, drain off any liquid, let cool, and shred.

SLOW COOKER METHOD

Season the beef with salt and pepper. Heat the oil in a large skillet over medium-high heat, then brown the meat. Place the beef, broth, onion, garlic, and bay leaves in the slow cooker and cook on high for 4 hours. Remove the meat from the pot, drain off any liquid, let cool, and shred.

Freezer Friendly: Place into an airtight container and freeze for up to 3 months.

Beef & Pea Stroganoff

After getting a bit bored with the same old stroganoff recipe, I came up with this version. My first trick is using juicy sirloin instead of a stew meat that requires hours of simmering to tenderize. That swap alone makes this version a winner, because it can go from fridge to fork in just 40 minutes with maximum flavor.

The next change-up is in the sauce. And here is a secret I've never revealed: I put onion soup mix in the gravy. I still add smoked paprika, black pepper, and parsley, but the soup seasoning adds loads of flavor with little effort. Mushrooms soak up all of the sweet goodness from the sherry wine, although if you wanted to swap that out with beef broth, be my guest.

PREP TIME | 10 minutes   COOK TIME | 30 minutes   SERVES | 4

½ cup all-purpose flour

1½ pounds top sirloin, trimmed and cut against the grain into ½-inch-thick strips

1 tablespoon vegetable oil

½ cup cooking sherry

1 cup chopped white onion

2 cups sliced white mushrooms

2 teaspoons Dijon mustard

1½ cups low-sodium beef broth

1 (1-ounce) envelope onion soup mix

1 tablespoon dried parsley

1 teaspoon smoked paprika

½ teaspoon freshly ground black pepper

½ cup heavy cream

1 cup frozen peas

2 teaspoons cornstarch (optional)

¼ cup water (optional)

12 ounces dry egg noodles

2 tablespoons unsalted butter

1 Pour the flour into a medium bowl. Toss the beef in the flour, shake off the excess, and place the floured strips on a plate.

2 Heat the oil in a large skillet over medium-high heat. Add the beef, working in two batches so as not to crowd the skillet. Brown the strips, then transfer to another plate.

3 Using the same skillet, pour in the sherry and stir to deglaze all the browned bits. Add the onion and mushrooms, and cook for 4 to 5 minutes, or until the liquid is nearly absorbed and the mushrooms have shrunk by half. Whisk in the mustard, then add the broth, soup mix, parsley, paprika, and pepper. Mix well and return the beef to the skillet. Reduce heat to low and simmer for 5 minutes, letting the flavors marry.

4 Stir in the cream and peas, heating for 5 minutes. If the sauce isn't thick enough for your liking, whisk together the cornstarch and water in a small bowl, add the paste to the sauce, then remove the skillet from the heat. The sauce will thicken in 2 to 3 minutes.

5 Meanwhile, as the beef and sauce simmer and heat, cook the noodles according to package directions until al dente. Drain and toss with the butter.

6 Serve the beef strips and stroganoff sauce over the buttered egg noodles.

Shepherd's Pie Mac & Cheese

Old-school shepherd's pie features a layer of seasoned chopped or ground lamb and vegetables covered by wispy mashed potatoes. In the United States, beef is usually substituted for lamb. I decided to ditch the potatoes and invert the whole recipe to put the main ingredient on top of a mound of silky mac and cheese with a crunchy topping for added interest. While the ingredient list looks long, the ingredients are kitchen staples, and several are used in both layers.

PREP TIME | 15 minutes   COOK TIME | 40 minutes   SERVES | 6

FOR THE BEEF

- 1 tablespoon vegetable oil
- ½ cup minced carrot
- ½ cup minced celery
- ½ white onion, chopped
- 2 garlic cloves, minced
- 1 pound 90% lean ground beef
- ¼ cup low-sodium beef broth
- 1 tablespoon Worcestershire sauce
- 1 tablespoon tomato paste
- ½ teaspoon freshly ground black pepper
- ½ teaspoon kosher salt
- ½ teaspoon dried rosemary
- ½ teaspoon dried thyme
- ½ cup frozen corn
- ½ cup frozen peas

FOR THE MAC AND CHEESE

- ½ pound elbow macaroni
- 2 tablespoons unsalted butter
- 2 tablespoons all-purpose flour
- 1½ cups whole milk
- 1½ cups shredded Gruyère cheese
- ½ teaspoon kosher salt
- ½ teaspoon freshly ground black pepper

FOR THE TOPPING

- ¼ cup panko
- ½ teaspoon dried rubbed sage
- ¼ teaspoon freshly ground black pepper
- ¼ teaspoon kosher salt

1 **Make the beef:** Heat the oil in a large skillet over medium heat. Add the carrot, celery, onion, and garlic, sautéing until they start to soften, 4 to 5 minutes.

2 Add the beef and cook, breaking it apart and turning, until no pink remains, about 5 minutes. Add the broth, Worcestershire, tomato paste, pepper, salt, rosemary, and thyme to the skillet. Stir well and reduce the heat to low. Simmer until most of the liquid is gone, then add the corn and peas. Toss to combine, then remove the skillet from the heat. The residual heat will thaw the vegetables.

3 **Make the mac and cheese:** Cook the pasta according to package directions for al dente. Drain and set aside in a separate bowl.

4 In the pasta pot, melt the butter over medium heat. Whisk in the flour to make a paste, then whisk in the milk until the flour has dissolved. Add the cheese and stir until thoroughly melted and smooth. Remove from the heat and season with the salt and pepper. Fold the cooked pasta into the sauce.

5 **Make the topping:** Preheat the oven to 350°F (180°C). Combine the panko, sage, pepper, and salt in a small bowl.

6 In an ovenproof skillet or 9- by 13-inch baking dish, spread out the mac and cheese, top with the shepherd's pie filling, then sprinkle with the seasoned panko. Bake, uncovered, for 10 minutes. Serve hot.

Freezer Friendly: This one-dish meal can be frozen right in the casserole dish, covered tightly with aluminum foil. Freeze for up to 3 months. To reheat, place the covered dish in a 350°F (180°C) oven and bake for 30 to 40 minutes, or until the center registers 165°F (75°C) on an instant-read thermometer.

Cook's Notes | To shave time from the prep, use 90% lean ground beef to avoid having to drain it. Cook the pasta while the meat is browning.

Gruyère cheese can be swapped out for fontina, white cheddar, or smoked Gouda. A 6-ounce block of cheese equals 1½ cups shredded.

Not Your Momma's Meatloaf

Meatloaf should be juicy, flavorful, and an all-around comfort food, not a dry, tasteless brick of ground beef. It also shouldn't taste like a hamburger or a meatball. To achieve the perfect meatloaf, you'll need to start with ground beef that has a good amount of fat to keep it moist and to add flavor. A leaner blend is likely to get tough when cooked.

I also sneak veggies into the mix after grating or mincing them so they blend uniformly into the texture. Evaporated milk provides moisture and helps the breadcrumbs swell and turn into little flavor bombs. Combine this with freshly shredded cheddar cheese, spices, and an amazingly tangy topping, and you've got yourself a winning meatloaf!

I doubt you'll have leftovers, but if you do, expect an outstanding cold meatloaf sandwich.

PREP TIME | 15 minutes   **COOK TIME** | 55 minutes   **SERVES** | 4

- 1 cup seasoned breadcrumbs
- ½ cup finely minced or grated white onion
- ½ cup finely minced or grated carrot
- ½ cup evaporated milk
- ½ cup shredded cheddar cheese
- 1 garlic clove, finely minced
- ½ cup plus 2 tablespoons ketchup
- 1 tablespoon Worcestershire sauce
- 1 egg, lightly beaten
- ½ teaspoon kosher salt
- ½ teaspoon freshly ground black pepper
- ¾ teaspoon garlic powder
- 1 pound 80% lean ground beef, broken into small pieces
- 2 tablespoons firmly packed light brown sugar
- 1 tablespoon red wine vinegar
- ¼ teaspoon onion powder
  Mashed potatoes, rice, or egg noodles, for serving

1 Preheat the oven to 350°F (180°C). Coat a meatloaf pan or standard bread loaf pan with cooking spray.

2 Combine the breadcrumbs, onion, carrot, milk, cheese, garlic, 2 tablespoons of the ketchup, the Worcestershire, egg, salt, pepper, and ½ teaspoon of the garlic powder in a large bowl. Mix into a paste. Add the beef, blending until just combined. Try not to overmix. Transfer the beef mixture to the prepared pan.

3 Stir together the remaining ½ cup ketchup, the sugar, vinegar, onion powder, and remaining ¼ teaspoon of garlic powder in a small bowl. Mix well, then slather the mixture over the meatloaf, spreading to the edges.

4 Bake for 55 minutes, or until the internal temperature reaches 155°F (68°C).

5 Allow the meatloaf to sit for 5 to 10 minutes before slicing and serving with mashed potatoes, rice, or egg noodles.

Meatloaf Tricks

- I highly recommend using a meatloaf pan. It looks like a standard bread loaf pan but has a little shelf that lets excess fat drip out the bottom.

- For zesty or spicy meatloaf, substitute an equal amount of your favorite barbecue sauce or chunky salsa for the ketchup.

- Instead of cheddar, use smoked Gouda, pepper Jack, or another medium-textured brick cheese.

- Evaporated milk can be swapped for whole milk. Do not use sweetened condensed milk (a common mistake); it's the same as evaporated but with a lot of sugar!

- If you don't have seasoned breadcrumbs, add 1 tablespoon Italian seasoning to plain breadcrumbs or panko.

Cube Steak with Mushroom Gravy
and Crispy Fried Onions

Like ground beef, cube steak isn't an actual cut of beef but a preparation. Thin cuts trimmed from other pieces are run through a tenderizer that gives the meat its characteristic cubed appearance. Because they are quite lean, cube steaks are best cooked with quick, high heat and some sauce to help keep them juicy. Although this type of meat is often used for chicken-fried steak, "cube steak" is its own recipe, typically served with a brown gravy over potatoes, egg noodles, or rice.

This version uses a shortcut of onion soup mix along with fresh mushrooms. Seasoned flour helps thicken the sauce, and purchased crispy fried onions tossed on top give the whole dish texture and allure.

PREP TIME | 5 minutes   COOK TIME | 15 minutes   SERVES | 4

½ cup all-purpose flour

½ teaspoon garlic powder

½ teaspoon onion powder

½ teaspoon smoked paprika

½ teaspoon kosher salt

½ teaspoon freshly ground black pepper

1 tablespoon vegetable oil

4 cube steaks (approximately 1½ pounds)

2 tablespoons unsalted butter

2 cups sliced white mushrooms

1 teaspoon Dijon mustard

1½ cups low-sodium beef broth

1 (1-ounce) envelope onion soup mix

Mashed potatoes, rice, or egg noodles, for serving

1 cup crispy fried onions

1. Stir together the flour, garlic powder, onion powder, paprika, salt, and pepper in a shallow bowl. Reserve 1 tablespoon.

2. Heat the oil in a large skillet over medium heat.

3. Dredge the cube steaks in the flour mixture, shaking off the excess. Cook each steak for 3 minutes on each side, or until browned. Transfer the steaks to a plate, leaving behind the browned bits.

4. Add the butter and mushrooms to the skillet, tossing the mushrooms until soft and reduced in size by half, about 5 minutes. Clear a little spot in the corner of the skillet and add the 1 tablespoon reserved flour and the mustard, stirring them into a paste. Then incorporate the mushrooms. Slowly add the broth, stirring until smooth. Stir in the soup mix, then simmer over medium heat for 3 to 4 minutes.

5. Return the beef to the skillet, turning to coat. Simmer for 2 minutes longer. The gravy should have thickened enough to coat the back of a spoon.

6. Serve over mashed potatoes, rice, or egg noodles. Top with crispy fried onions.

Beer & Onion Braised Brisket

Brisket is best prepared with moist heat (or smoked with dry heat). Some regard brisket as one of the trickiest cuts of beef to cook properly because it requires extra work to make it supertender. This simple version requires little hands-on time and produces excellent results. Braising is usually done in the oven, but here we keep it on the stovetop using superlow heat so the liquid barely simmers instead of boils. While the meat has a good amount of flavor on its own, I like pairing it with my favorite barbecue sauce. Leftovers are great in a grilled cheese sandwich or quesadilla, or even on a pizza or nachos.

PREP TIME | 10 minutes   **COOK TIME** | 3 hours 45 minutes   **SERVES** | 8

- 5 pounds untrimmed flat cut brisket
- 2 teaspoons kosher salt
- 1 teaspoon freshly ground black pepper
- 2 tablespoons vegetable oil
- 2 large white onions, cut into eighths
- 4 garlic cloves, minced
- 2 teaspoons dry mustard
- 2 teaspoons dried thyme leaves
- 16 ounces dark beer, such as a porter or dark lager
- 1 cup low-sodium beef broth
  Barbecue sauce, for serving (optional)

1 Season both sides of the brisket with the salt and pepper, rubbing them in well. You may need to cut the meat into two or three pieces to make it easier to work with and fit into your pot for browning.

2 Heat the oil in a large pot over medium-high heat. Brown the brisket on all sides. Work in batches, if needed. Remove the meat from the pot and set aside.

3 With the oil still in the pot, add the onions, garlic, mustard, thyme, beer, and broth to the pot and bring to a low boil. Reduce the heat to the lowest setting on your stovetop; you might even want to transfer the pot to the smallest burner. Return the meat to the pot. The liquid might not fully cover the meat, and that is fine.

4 Cover and braise for 3 hours, moving pieces around every hour to make sure everything gets an equal amount of time submerged.

5 Using tongs, transfer the beef to a cutting board and cut it against the grain into thin strips. Using a slotted spoon, serve the onions over the beef slices. Serve with barbecue sauce, if desired.

Flavorful Fork-Tender Pot Roast

Long gone are the days of leathery, chewy pot roast. The proper technique turns a piece of chuck into a well-cooked, fork-tender roast that any chef would be proud to serve. Here the secret ingredient is acidic tomato sauce to help tenderize the beef, not to mention enrich the gravy.

Oven braising is the most traditional method of preparation, but I've included easy instructions for using the electric pressure cooker and slow cooker to get the same results. No matter which technique you use, don't skip the browning—it is key to a flavorful pot roast!

PREP TIME | 20 minutes   **COOK TIME** | 4 hours 30 minutes   **SERVES** | 6

1 tablespoon vegetable oil

4–5 pounds chuck roast

1 teaspoon kosher salt

½ teaspoon freshly ground black pepper

4 carrots, ends trimmed and cut into 2-inch pieces

4 red potatoes, scrubbed and quartered

3 celery stalks, trimmed and cut into 2-inch pieces

1 yellow onion, peeled and quartered

2 garlic cloves, finely minced or pressed

1 (10-ounce) can plain tomato sauce

2 cups low-sodium beef broth

1 tablespoon red wine vinegar

1 tablespoon Italian seasoning

2 tablespoons cornstarch

½ cup cold water

1. Arrange an oven rack in the lower-third position and preheat the oven to 275°F (135°C).

2. Heat the oil in a large cast-iron pot or Dutch oven (at least 6 quarts) over medium-high heat. Blot the roast dry with paper towels, season with the salt and pepper, and sear the beef in the pot, until well browned. Turn off the stovetop and arrange the carrots, potatoes, celery, onion, and garlic around the roast. Pour in the tomato sauce, broth, and vinegar, add the Italian seasoning, and toss to coat everything in liquid.

3. Cover and braise in the oven for 4 hours.

4. Remove the vegetables and meat from the pot using a slotted spoon. Skim any fat from the liquid. Place the pot on the stove over medium heat and bring the liquid to a simmer. As it heats, whisk together the cornstarch and water in a small bowl, then pour this paste into the pot. Whisk until the gravy begins to thicken. Remove the pot from the heat.

5. Use two forks to break the roast into chunks. Drizzle gravy over each serving of meat and vegetables.

Continued on next page

Flavorful Fork-Tender Pot Roast, *continued*

PRESSURE COOKER METHOD

Use a 3-pound roast for a 6-quart cooker and a 4- to 5-pound roast for a 9-quart cooker. Set the electric pressure cooker to the sauté function, then heat the oil. Cut the roast into six or seven large pieces, browning each in the pot. Add the carrots, potatoes, celery, onion, garlic, tomato sauce, broth, vinegar, and Italian seasoning.

Seal the lid and set the cooker to manual high pressure for 50 minutes. Use the quick release function, then remove the meat and the vegetables. Set the cooker on sauté, and skim any fat. Whisk together the cornstarch and water in a small bowl and add this paste to the broth. Allow the gravy to thicken, then serve.

SLOW COOKER METHOD

Brown the meat in a separate skillet and transfer to the slow cooker. Add the carrots, potatoes, celery, onion, garlic, tomato sauce, broth, vinegar, and Italian seasoning. Place the lid on and cook the roast on high for 4 hours.

Remove the meat and vegetables, and skim any fat. Whisk together the cornstarch and water in a small bowl and add this paste to the broth. Allow the gravy to thicken, then serve.

Super Stuffed Peppers

The classic combo of ground beef and rice packed into a green bell pepper seems a little humdrum, don't you think? Everyone loves a colorful meal, so start by using one of the rainbow colors of sweet peppers available: red, yellow, orange, even purple! A splash of balsamic vinegar blends with the tomato juices into a sweet glaze. It is just enough to make this dish flavorful without being overwhelming.

PREP TIME | 15 minutes   COOK TIME | 35 minutes   SERVES | 6

1 tablespoon vegetable oil

1 pound 80% lean ground beef

¼ cup low-sodium beef broth

½ cup chopped white onion

1 garlic clove, minced

1 cup cooked long-grain rice

½ cup petite diced tomatoes, drained

2 tablespoons balsamic vinegar

2 tablespoons chopped fresh Italian parsley

2 teaspoons Italian seasoning

¼ teaspoon kosher salt

¼ teaspoon freshly ground black pepper

6 large bell peppers, assorted colors, cut in half lengthwise, membranes and seeds discarded

¾ cup shredded mozzarella cheese

1 cup marinara sauce

1 Preheat the oven to 350°F (180°C). Coat a 9- by 13-inch baking dish with cooking spray.

2 Heat the oil in a large skillet over medium heat. Add the beef, breaking it apart as you cook. Add the broth to keep it moist. When the liquid has reduced by more than half, add the onion and garlic, and cook until soft.

3 When the beef is cooked through and the onion is soft (8 to 10 minutes), add the rice, tomatoes, vinegar, parsley, Italian seasoning, salt, and pepper, and cook until heated through, 3 to 4 minutes.

4 Spoon the beef filling into each bell pepper half, heaping up and out if you have more filling than will fit. Top with the cheese and marinara sauce. Bake, uncovered, for 20 minutes. Allow to sit for 5 minutes before serving.

Cook's Notes | Cutting the peppers horizontally allows you to pile the stuffing higher, making a dramatic appearance on the dinner table.

To make this recipe even quicker, grab a pouch of 90-second rice. It saves time, plus using a fun flavor like wild or butter and garlic adds more savory layers to your finished dish. Double win!

Sheet Pan Steak Fajitas

Skirt steak is the ultimate choice for fajitas—already a thin cut, it doesn't require much in the way of trimming to fit perfectly in a tortilla. The trick here is to cut the steak into three pieces before cooking. Then you can cut the meat across the grain to produce tender strips that don't put up a fight when you bite into them.

Fajitas are generally made on a flattop grill or in a really hot cast-iron pan. Using the oven reduces splatters and mess while keeping all the flavor.

PREP TIME | 15 minutes   **COOK TIME** | 20 minutes   **MAKES** | 10–12 fajitas

1 tablespoon sugar

2 teaspoons chili powder

1 teaspoon kosher salt

½ teaspoon garlic powder

½ teaspoon onion powder

½ teaspoon dried oregano

½ teaspoon ground cumin

¼ teaspoon freshly ground black pepper

3 bell peppers, seeded and cut into strips

1 white onion, thinly sliced

1 tablespoon vegetable oil

2 garlic cloves, grated

1 teaspoon lime zest

2 teaspoons lime juice

1½ pounds skirt steak, cut into 3 equal pieces

12 flour tortillas

OPTIONAL TOPPINGS

Avocado slices

Sour cream

Fresh cilantro

Jalapeño slices

Red onion, thinly sliced

1 Preheat the oven to 350°F (180°C). Line a large rimmed baking sheet with aluminum foil.

2 Stir together the sugar, chili powder, salt, garlic powder, onion powder, oregano, cumin, and black pepper in a small bowl. This is your fajita seasoning.

3 Combine the bell peppers, onion, and oil with half of the fajita seasoning in a large bowl. Toss well to coat. Pour the vegetables onto the prepared baking sheet. Bake for 10 minutes.

4 Meanwhile, stir the garlic, lime zest, and lime juice into the remaining fajita seasoning to make a paste. Slather the paste onto the top of each piece of steak.

5 Remove the pan of vegetables at 10 minutes. Set the oven broiler to high. Add the steak pieces to the pan, shuffling the vegetables around to accommodate the meat while keeping everything in a single layer. Broil for 5 to 7 minutes on the middle rack. *This time will vary greatly with each oven, so watch closely to ensure that the food doesn't burn.*

6 **Finish and top:** Allow the meat and veggies to rest in the pan for at least 5 minutes. Slice each piece of meat against the grain into thin strips, then serve on tortillas with your favorite fajita toppings.

Thai Coconut Beef with Coconut Sticky Rice

Accompanied by fresh, snappy veggies in a coconut-based sauce, this beef is hard to beat. It is a family favorite that comes together in a jiffy. I'm equally in love with the rice, which can be served with any Asian-inspired dish or by itself.

PREP TIME | 15 minutes   COOK TIME | 45 minutes   SERVES | 4

FOR THE BEEF

- 3 tablespoons cornstarch
- ½ teaspoon kosher salt
- ½ teaspoon freshly ground black pepper
- 1½ pounds top sirloin, cut against the grain into ½-inch strips
- 2 tablespoons vegetable oil
- 1 small yellow onion, quartered
- 1 red bell pepper, seeded and cut into strips
- 1 cup fresh sugar snap peas
- 1 tablespoon grated fresh ginger
- 1 garlic clove, grated
- 2 cups coconut milk
- 1–2 tablespoons garlic chile sauce
- 1 tablespoon sugar
- 1 tablespoon lime juice
- ¼ packed cup whole Thai basil leaves

FOR THE RICE

- 2 cups dry jasmine rice
- 1 cup water
- 1 cup coconut milk
- 1 tablespoon lime juice
- ½ teaspoon lime zest
- ½ teaspoon kosher salt
- 1 tablespoon sugar

1 **Make the beef:** Combine the cornstarch, salt, and black pepper in a medium bowl. Toss with the beef.

2 Heat 1 tablespoon of the oil in a large skillet or cast-iron pan over medium-high heat. Working in two batches, brown the beef. Remove and set aside.

3 In the same skillet, add the remaining 1 tablespoon oil along with the onion, bell pepper, and peas. Cook over medium-high heat for 5 minutes, or until lightly browned. The onions *will not* be fully soft or opaque. Stir in the ginger and garlic, and cook for 1 minute.

4 Add the coconut milk, garlic chile sauce, sugar, and lime juice, and return the beef to the skillet, spooning the sauce over the meat to coat. Simmer over low heat for 5 to 7 minutes, or until the sauce starts to combine and thicken.

5 **Make the rice:** In a fine-mesh sieve or colander, rinse the rice until the water runs clear.

6 Stir together the rice, water, coconut milk, lime juice, lime zest, salt, and sugar in a large saucepan. Bring to a full boil, then cover and reduce the heat to low. Cook for 25 to 30 minutes without opening the lid.

7 **Finish the dish:** Right before serving, stir the basil into the beef mixture. Remove the rice saucepan's lid and fluff the rice with a fork. Serve the meat and sauce over the rice.

> **Cook's Notes |** Thai basil looks similar to sweet Italian basil but has a different flavor profile. It is rich, savory, and a little spicy. Some compare the taste to black licorice or anise. If you can't find it, sweet basil is an option, but the basil can also be omitted and you'll still have a winning dish.
>
> If you start the rice first, it will be done at the same time as the beef. But if cooking rice from scratch isn't in the cards, pick up two bags of microwavable jasmine rice and call it a night.

Snappy Bolognese Sauce

Bolognese sauce is simply a hearty Italian sauce made with ground beef and vegetables. The sauce itself is tomato based but commonly includes cheese, milk, or cream as well as wine. The robust flavors need time to marry, so while the active time is less than 30 minutes, the sauce itself needs an hour or so to simmer and reduce. Instead of adding wine, I use just a splash of red wine vinegar to add a similar acidity. This tasty mixture can be served over pasta, used as a meat sauce in lasagna, or incorporated in any meal that begs for a tomato-based sauce.

PREP TIME | 20 minutes   **COOK TIME** | 1 hour 30 minutes   **SERVES** | 6

- 1 tablespoon extra-virgin olive oil
- 1 pound 80% lean ground beef
- 1 cup chopped white onion
- ½ cup chopped carrots
- ½ cup chopped celery
- 3 garlic cloves, minced
- 1 (28-ounce) can crushed tomatoes
- 1 cup water
- 2 tablespoons tomato paste
- 6 large fresh basil leaves, finely minced
- 1 tablespoon red wine vinegar
- 2 teaspoons sugar
- ½ cup heavy cream
- ½ teaspoon freshly ground black pepper
- 1 pound pasta, cooked al dente
  Parmesan cheese, for topping

1. Heat the oil in a large pot over high heat. Add the beef, breaking it into pieces in the pot. Brown on all sides. Drain the beef and set aside.

2. Without rinsing the pot, return it to the burner and reduce the heat to medium. Add the onion, carrots, celery, and garlic. Sweat the vegetables for 5 minutes, stirring to coat. They will still be firm.

3. Add the crushed tomatoes, water, tomato paste, basil, vinegar, and sugar. Simmer for 1 hour over low heat, stirring occasionally. The mixture should thicken, reduce, and darken in color.

4. Right before serving, stir in the cream and pepper. Serve over your favorite pasta with freshly grated Parmesan.

Freezer Friendly: I encourage you to make a double, or even triple, batch. Freeze in an airtight container for up to 3 months.

Cook's Note | To add even more flavor, add 1 or 2 links of hot Italian sausage, meat removed from the casing and crumbled, to the ground beef mixture.

Sweet & Spicy Mongolian Beef

Mongolian beef is a Chinese restaurant favorite that tends to land on the sweet side. I prefer it with a little heat for balance. The amount of chile can be easily adjusted, from slightly spicy to so hot it makes you sweat.

I use a single red cayenne chile, which is *hot*! Use a less-intense chile like jalapeño or even just a dash of red pepper flakes to dial back the heat. Omit the chile altogether for a more traditional sweet dish.

Serve with plain white rice or jazz it up with Coconut Sticky Rice (page 89).

PREP TIME | 20 minutes   COOK TIME | 15 minutes   SERVES | 4

¼ cup cornstarch

½ teaspoon kosher salt

1½ pounds flank steak, cut against the grain into thin strips

2 tablespoons vegetable oil

2 cups trimmed and cut broccoli florets

½ white onion, thinly sliced

1 tablespoon grated fresh ginger

1 garlic clove, finely minced

⅔ cup firmly packed light brown sugar

½ cup low-sodium soy sauce

½ cup water

1 red cayenne chile, seeded and cut into rings

4 cups cooked white rice

2 teaspoons toasted sesame seeds, for serving

1 chopped scallion, for serving

1 Combine the cornstarch and salt in a medium bowl. Toss the beef in the cornstarch mixture, tapping off the excess and setting the meat on a separate plate. Allow to sit for 10 minutes.

2 Meanwhile, heat 1 tablespoon of the vegetable oil in a large skillet or wok over medium-high heat. Add the broccoli, onion, ginger, and garlic. Sauté for 5 minutes, or until the onion starts to soften and the broccoli turns a brilliant green but they both still have snap. Add the sugar, soy sauce, water, and chile, stirring to combine. Reduce heat to low and bring to a simmer, then transfer the veggies and liquid to a heatproof bowl.

3 In the same skillet, heat the remaining 1 tablespoon oil over medium-high heat. Working in two batches, cook the beef for 2 to 3 minutes on each side, until browned. Return all the beef, sauce, and vegetables to the hot skillet, maintaining the medium-high heat. Toss to coat.

4 The sauce will thicken in 3 to 4 minutes. Remove from the heat and serve over the rice. Garnish with the sesame seeds and scallion.

Cook's Note | The process of dipping a protein in cornstarch and allowing it to sit before cooking is called velveting. Cornstarch creates a barrier that keeps moisture in while the meat browns. Letting the cornstarch set properly and then cooking with a quick, hot sear are the keys to making sure it stays smooth without getting gummy. The cornstarch also helps thicken the sauce.

Caramelized Onion Salisbury Steak

This nostalgic recipe uses only a handful of kitchen staples. The trick to a full-bodied Salisbury steak is to properly brown the beef patties and mushrooms and to slowly caramelize the onions. Doing so creates a rich, sophisticated gravy with tender, juicy patties. The other secret ingredient is, believe it or not, onion soup mix. I love it because it adds extra beef flavor and seasonings without calling for more work or a long list of ingredients. Serve over mashed potatoes, broad egg noodles, or rice.

PREP TIME | 10 minutes   **COOK TIME** | 50 minutes   **SERVES** | 4

FOR THE PATTIES

- ½ cup seasoned breadcrumbs
- 2 tablespoons ketchup
- 1 tablespoon Worcestershire sauce
- 1 teaspoon Dijon mustard
- 1 egg
- ½ teaspoon kosher salt
- ½ teaspoon freshly ground black pepper
- 1 pound 80% lean ground beef
- 1 tablespoon vegetable oil

FOR THE GRAVY

- 2 tablespoons unsalted butter
- ½ white onion, cut into rings
- 8 ounces white mushrooms, thinly sliced
- 2½ cups low-sodium beef broth
- 1 tablespoon ketchup
- 1 tablespoon Dijon mustard
- 1 tablespoon Worcestershire sauce
- 1 (1-ounce) envelope onion soup mix
- 1 tablespoon cornstarch
- 1 tablespoon water
- Mashed potatoes, egg noodles, or rice, for serving

1 **Make the patties:** Mix together the breadcrumbs, ketchup, Worcestershire, mustard, egg, salt, and pepper in a medium bowl until a paste forms. Add the beef, breaking it into pieces. Toss the mixture with your hands to combine, then form it into four equal-size patties with a well in the center of each. Avoid overmixing.

2 Heat the oil in a large skillet over medium-high heat. Add the patties, browning well until a crust forms on both sides, 3 to 4 minutes per side. Remove the patties from the skillet and set aside.

3 **Make the gravy:** Reduce the heat to medium-low and add 1 tablespoon of the butter and the onion to the skillet. Stirring occasionally, brown the onions for 20 to 25 minutes, until they reach a light caramel color. Add the mushrooms and remaining 1 tablespoon butter, increase the heat to medium-high, and cook for 5 to 8 minutes, or until the mushrooms are reduced in size by half. Stir in the broth, ketchup, mustard, Worcestershire, and soup mix, then bring to a low simmer.

4 Combine the cornstarch and water in a small bowl until a paste forms. Whisk this paste into the brown gravy mixture.

5 Return the beef patties to the gravy, turning them to coat. Reduce the heat to low and cook for 5 minutes longer, or until the gravy has thickened.

6 Serve over mashed potatoes, egg noodles, or rice.

Cook's Note | Creating a well in the center of each patty keeps them flat as they cook, so they don't mound up as the fibers shrink. It also helps you resist the urge to flatten the patties with a spatula, which would press out all the juices.

Gouda-Stuffed Flank Steak

My dinner-party options increased tremendously when I realized I could stuff and roll a flank steak to serve up to six people. A stuffed roll of meat looks impressive and tastes phenomenal, and the stuffing combinations are nearly endless. Flank steak is a relatively lean cut and can be tough. Because this roast isn't marinated, the tenderizing process takes place manually with a meat mallet. The tough fibers are further broken down by rolling and slicing the meat against the grain.

| PREP TIME | 20 minutes | COOK TIME | 1 hour | SERVES | 6 |

- 1 tablespoon unsalted butter
- ⅓ cup roughly chopped white mushrooms
- 1 heaping tablespoon chopped white onion
- 1 garlic clove, minced
- 1 cup fresh spinach, packed
- 1½ pounds flank steak
- ½ teaspoon kosher salt
- ½ teaspoon freshly ground black pepper
- ½ cup shredded smoked Gouda
- 1 tablespoon vegetable oil

Cook's Notes | My favorite part of this recipe is the smoked Gouda, which gives a magical flavor and aroma. If you can't find it, use another smoked cheese such as Havarti, Munster, or even white cheddar. Any leftovers will make a killer grilled cheese sandwich.

If you are worried about butterflying the steak, ask your butcher to do it for you. Most butchers are quite happy to open the package, cut it quick, and then repackage it.

You can stuff and tie the roast ahead of time and place it in the refrigerator for up to a day before cooking. You can even brown it in advance, then roast right before serving. If you do this, add 5 minutes to the roasting time to account for the meat being chilled.

1 Preheat the oven to 350°F (180°C).

2 Heat a large skillet over medium heat. Add the butter, mushrooms, and onion, and sauté until the vegetables are reduced in size and browned, 5 to 8 minutes. Add the garlic and spinach, and, using tongs, toss until the spinach is wilted. Transfer the vegetables to a medium bowl and turn off the heat, but leave the skillet out to use in step 5.

3 Place the steak on a cutting board. Using a sharp chef's knife, butterfly the steak so that it can be opened like a book, leaving the "back binding" intact. The easiest way to do this is to place one hand on top of the meat and hold it down tightly while slicing directly through the center without cutting all the way through. Leave the two halves connected but cut enough so that you can open them. Tenderize the meat using the textured side of a meat mallet to create uniform thickness.

4 Sprinkle the meat surface with the salt and pepper. Evenly spread out the spinach mixture, then top with the cheese. Starting from the shorter side, tightly roll up the flank steak. Secure it by tying it with three or four pieces of butcher's twine.

5 Heat the oil over high heat in the skillet. Brown the rolled beef for 2 to 3 minutes per side, until the surface is evenly cooked.

6 Transfer the meat to a rimmed baking sheet. Bake, uncovered, for 35 to 40 minutes. For medium doneness, the center should register at least 145°F (63°C). Cooking times will vary depending on the thickness of the beef roll.

7 Allow the roast to rest for 10 minutes before slicing and serving.

Creamy 40-Clove Garlic Beef

You may be familiar with 40-clove chicken, a version of a traditional French dish that uses amazing caramelized garlic in a comforting cream sauce. I figured, "Why not try it with beef?" Tender top sirloin and fresh herbs work beautifully with the garlic, which is gently cooked to enhance the flavor without being overpowering. The traditional accompaniment is mashed potatoes, but pasta or rice are also excellent choices, as is a slice of crusty bread to sop up every bit of the sauce.

PREP TIME | 20 minutes   COOK TIME | 45 minutes   SERVES | 4

- 1 tablespoon vegetable oil
- 1½ pounds top sirloin, trimmed and cut into bite-size pieces
- ½ teaspoon kosher salt
- ½ teaspoon freshly ground black pepper
- 2 tablespoons unsalted butter
- 40 garlic cloves, peeled
- 2½ cups low-sodium chicken broth
- 2 teaspoons fresh thyme leaves
- 2 teaspoons minced fresh rosemary
- 2 tablespoons all-purpose flour
- 2 tablespoons heavy cream
- 4 cups cooked white rice

1. Heat the oil in a large skillet over medium-high heat.

2. Toss the beef with the salt and pepper. Add the beef to the hot skillet, browning it evenly. Transfer it to a paper towel–lined plate. Reduce the heat to medium.

3. Wipe any residual liquids from the skillet. Add the butter and garlic cloves, and sauté until browned and fragrant, 6 to 7 minutes. Stir in 2 cups of the broth, the thyme, and rosemary. Simmer over low heat for 25 minutes, stirring occasionally.

4. Whisk together the flour and cream in a small bowl until a paste forms. Stir in the remaining ½ cup broth, whisking until smooth.

5. Return the beef to the skillet with the garlic and toss to heat. Turn off the heat, add the cream sauce to the hot skillet, and toss. The sauce will immediately thicken.

6. Serve the beef and sauce over the rice.

Cook's Note | Garlic's potency changes depending on how many membranes are ruptured and how much surface area is exposed. Pressed or sliced garlic is more intense when cooked, but whole cloves caramelized in butter and broth become deliciously fragrant and flavorful.

Cheesy Baked Burritos

Yay, it's burrito night! Everybody eats a little too much when these are on the menu. This is a good recipe for using leftover cooked beef, if you have enough on hand. I prefer my Easy Shredded Beef (page 72), but ground beef or cube steak works fine.

Using chunky salsa or pico de gallo is another time-saving hack. Instead of chopping bell peppers, onion, and tomato and then cooking them all down, choose a thick salsa that won't add too much liquid to the mix. I add corn and sometimes even a can of black beans, but both are optional. Just don't skimp on the beef or the cheese!

PREP TIME | 15 minutes　　COOK TIME | 15 minutes　　SERVES | 8

2½ cups cooked beef, ground, shredded, or cubed

1 cup thick and chunky salsa or pico de gallo

½ cup corn, drained or thawed (optional)

½ cup canned black or pinto beans, rinsed and drained (optional)

1½ cups shredded cheddar cheese

8 large flour tortillas

1 cup enchilada sauce

Sour cream, avocado slices, shredded iceberg lettuce, jalapeño slices, for topping (optional)

1　Preheat the oven to 350°F (180°C). Coat a 9- by 13-inch baking dish with cooking spray.

2　Toss together the beef, salsa, corn (if using), beans (if using), and 1 cup of the cheese in a large bowl.

3　Laying out one tortilla at a time on a large cutting board, place a scant ¾ cup of the beef mixture on the tortilla. Roll the tortilla tightly and place into the prepared baking dish seam side down. Repeat with the remaining tortillas.

4　Pour the enchilada sauce over the top and sprinkle with the remaining ½ cup cheese. Bake for 15 to 20 minutes, or until the cheese is hot and bubbly. Serve topped with sour cream, avocado, lettuce, and jalapeño, if desired, or your favorite burrito toppings.

Peanut-Beef Pad Thai

When I tell you that you may never order pad Thai at a restaurant again, I am not kidding. This recipe is *that* good and can be made with any protein, but obviously beef is my favorite. (Shrimp is a close second.) Many pad Thai recipes call for tamarind paste, a slightly acidic and sweet ingredient that I don't keep on hand because I don't use it in any other recipes. My version skips the tamarind paste but provides just as much flavor.

PREP TIME | 15 minutes   COOK TIME | 15 minutes   SERVES | 4

⅓ cup low-sodium chicken broth

3 tablespoons firmly packed light brown sugar

2 tablespoons rice wine vinegar

2 tablespoons fish sauce

2 heaping tablespoons creamy peanut butter

1 tablespoon low-sodium soy sauce

1 tablespoon lime juice

1 (14-ounce) package stir-fry rice noodles

3 teaspoons vegetable oil

1½ pounds top sirloin, cut against the grain into thin 2-inch pieces

1 teaspoon kosher salt

1 cup fresh sugar snap peas

½ red bell pepper, thinly sliced

½ cup shredded carrots

1 egg

1 cup fresh cilantro leaves

½ cup dry-roasted peanuts

4 scallions, whites only, chopped

Lime wedges, for serving

1 Whisk together the broth, sugar, vinegar, fish sauce, peanut butter, soy sauce, and lime juice in a bowl until smooth. Set aside.

2 Cook the noodles according to package directions for al dente. Drain and rinse with cold water to stop the cooking process. Toss with 1 teaspoon of the oil to prevent sticking. Set aside.

3 Season the beef with the salt. Heat another 1 teaspoon of the oil in a large skillet over medium-high heat. Brown the beef on all sides, about 5 minutes. Transfer the beef to a plate. Pour off any liquid and wipe the skillet with a paper towel.

4 Add the remaining 1 teaspoon oil to the skillet and reduce the heat to medium. Stir in the sugar snap peas and cook for 2 to 3 minutes. Add the bell pepper and carrots, and cook for 2 to 3 minutes longer.

5 Move the vegetables to one side of the skillet and crack the egg in the empty side. Using a spatula, scramble the egg right in the skillet until cooked, then mix it in with the vegetables. Return the beef to the skillet and pour the peanut sauce over the top. Toss in the rice noodles, coating all the ingredients well, and let everything heat through.

6 Divide the pad Thai among four serving bowls and top with the cilantro, peanuts, and scallions. Serve with lime wedges.

Cook's Note | Fish sauce adds a deep umami flavor to many dishes. If you don't have any in your pantry, you can use a little extra soy sauce instead.

6

Handhelds

Shredded, sliced, or ground, beef is the perfect protein to slap between two pieces of bread for a casual meal indoors or out. I could have written an entire book just about sandwiches that feature beef. I mean, there are cookbooks just about burgers! Quick cooking and totally delectable, these beefy bites will be on your regular rotation for lunches and dinners.

The Perfect Hamburger

No beef book would be complete without a discussion of the perfect hamburger patty, which begins and ends with high-quality ground beef. For an ultrajuicy burger, look for a blend made with short rib or sirloin with some fat content. Avoid lean ground beef or one made with cheaper cuts, which tend to be chewy when cooked. You can season with salt and pepper, but the real finesse is in properly forming the patty.

Carefully select a burger bun that will fit your patty size and ancillary toppings. I prefer a daintier sesame seed bun or potato roll for a plain burger but choose a hearty kaiser roll or brioche bun for a drippy bacon cheeseburger.

PREP TIME | 10 minutes active; 60 minutes to freeze
COOK TIME | 10 minutes   **MAKES** | 4 burgers

1 pound 80% lean ground beef
Fine sea salt and freshly ground black pepper
4 hamburger buns, toasted
Favorite burger toppings

1 Divide the beef into four equal pieces. Using clean hands, form them into patties. If you have a burger press, use it, otherwise, make a well in the center of each patty with the back of a spoon or your thumb.

2 Place the patties in the freezer for 1 hour before cooking. If you choose not to freeze before cooking, reduce the cooking times by 1 minute on each side.

3 Season with salt and pepper right before cooking, gently tapping them into the patties to stick.

On the grill: Heat a grill to medium-high heat and oil the grates. Place the patties over direct heat, grilling on each side for 3 to 4 minutes.

On the stovetop: Spray a skillet with cooking spray and heat over medium-high heat. Sear the patties on each side for 3 to 4 minutes.

4 Place each patty on a toasted bun and top with your favorite burger toppings.

Tips for Making an Awesome Burger

- For best results, use a blend no leaner than 80 percent lean.

- Do not overwork the meat, which can make it tough and dry.

- Make a well in the center of each patty or use a press with ridges to prevent mounding in the center.

- Freeze patties for an hour before cooking to help them set, which will produce a nice char on the outside with a medium center. However, it is not advised to completely refreeze previously frozen meat.

- Season the individual patties right before cooking. Otherwise, the salt will draw moisture from the meat.

- Cook quickly over high heat.

- Do not press down with a spatula—you'll lose all the precious juices!

Not-So-Philly Cheesesteak

Cheesesteaks are a touchy topic that in certain crowds can spark heated arguments. With the bread, toppings, and cheese selection up for discussion, the only thing we can all agree on is that if it isn't made in Philadelphia, then it is *not* a Philly cheesesteak.

Authentic sandwiches are made with chipped beef, a frozen ribeye that is run through a deli slicer for tender, thin, delicate ribbons of well-marbled beef, then sizzled on a flat grill. This method is a little challenging for the home cook, so I use a sirloin sliced as thinly as possible followed by a quick cook in the skillet.

You can argue if you like, but in my book, bell peppers, onions, and mushrooms are the only acceptable toppings. Hard-core cheesesteak connoisseurs will tell you that Cheez Whiz is the only way to go, but provolone comes in a close second. As for the bread, find a long, thin hoagie roll that is neither too fluffy nor too hard. Or eat it like I do, sans the bread. There's nothing wrong with a plate of shredded beef, sautéed veggies, and melted cheese!

PREP TIME | 10 minutes   **COOK TIME** | 15 minutes   **MAKES** | 4 sandwiches

1 tablespoon vegetable oil

1 green bell pepper, cut into thin strips

½ white onion, cut into thin strips

½ cup sliced white mushrooms

1 pound thin-cut sirloin, sliced against the grain into fine strips

½ teaspoon garlic powder

½ teaspoon freshly ground black pepper

¼ teaspoon kosher salt

8 slices provolone cheese

4 large hoagie rolls, split

1 Heat ½ tablespoon of the oil in a large skillet over medium heat. Add the bell pepper, onion, and mushrooms, and cook until the onions are soft, 5 to 6 minutes. Transfer to a plate.

2 Add the remaining ½ tablespoon oil to the skillet and increase the heat to medium-high. Add the beef and season with the garlic powder, black pepper, and salt. Toss to combine, then cook until brown, about 5 minutes.

3 Return the vegetables to the skillet and toss to combine them with the meat and reheat. Place slices of cheese over the mixture. Put the lid on the skillet until the cheese is melted, about 1 minute.

4 Divide the mixture among the rolls and serve with your favorite condiments.

Tuscan Sirloin Sandwiches

Top sirloin is a lean but relatively tender cut. Most butchers offer a thin cut that is ideal for sandwiches. I often find steak sandwiches hard to wrangle, so when I make my own, I cut the meat against the grain and very thin. You should be able to pull the fibers apart easily with just your fingers after cooking. This sandwich combines two of my family's favorite sauces as well as fresh leafy arugula and the tart flavor of sun-dried tomatoes, all on crusty sourdough.

PREP TIME | 10 minutes   **COOK TIME** | 10 minutes   **MAKES** | 2 open-face sandwiches

1 teaspoon Italian seasoning

½ teaspoon garlic powder

½ teaspoon onion powder

½ teaspoon kosher salt

½ pound top sirloin, thinly sliced

2 teaspoons extra-virgin olive oil

¼ cup Quick Garlic Aioli (page 132)

4 large slices sourdough bread, toasted

½ cup fresh arugula

¼ cup sun-dried tomatoes, drained and blotted, cut into small pieces

2 tablespoons Balsamic Glaze (page 134)

1 Blend together the Italian seasoning, garlic powder, onion powder, and salt in a small bowl. Rub onto the sirloin pieces.

2 Heat the oil in a large skillet over medium-high heat. Sear the sirloin pieces until brown, about 1 minute on each side. Remove and allow to rest for 2 to 3 minutes.

3 Spread the aioli onto two slices of toast.

4 Rub the arugula lightly between your palms to bring out the flavor, then divide equally among the sandwiches.

5 Cut the meat into bite-size pieces and pile onto the sandwich bottoms. Top with sun-dried tomatoes and balsamic glaze. Finish with the remaining bread slices, cut each sandwich in half, and serve.

Cook's Note | Rubbing greens such as arugula and kale between your palms before adding them to a salad or sandwich helps break down the fibers, making them easier to chew.

Slow Cooker Italian Beef Sandwiches

Italian beef sandwiches are a classic Chicago recipe that puts a spin on the also-classic French dip. My recipe adds tangy pepperoncini (borrowed from yet another classic, Mississippi pot roast) to the au jus and giardiniera of the Chicago version. It is basically a juicy pot roast with pickled vegetables and cheese.

Many slow cooker recipes require you to brown the meat before adding it. As a foodie, I understand the importance of browning to develop sophisticated acidic flavors, but as a busy mom, I sometimes just don't have the time. I've tested this recipe both ways and find that adding additional beef bouillon and Worcestershire sauce gives the au jus an extrabeefy punch without needing to sear the meat.

PREP TIME | 5 minutes   **COOK TIME** | 6 hours   **MAKES** | 8 sandwiches

1 (16-ounce) jar whole pepperoncini with juice, stems removed

½ cup low-sodium beef broth

1 garlic clove, minced

1 tablespoon Italian seasoning

1 tablespoon powdered beef bouillon

1 tablespoon Worcestershire sauce

½ teaspoon freshly ground black pepper

2–3 pounds chuck roast

16 slices Swiss cheese

8 large sub rolls, toasted

1 cup giardiniera, coarsely chopped

1 Stir together the pepperoncini with juice, broth, garlic, Italian seasoning, bouillon, Worcestershire, and black pepper in the slow cooker. Add the chuck roast, flipping it so it is evenly coated.

2 Cook for 6 hours on low. Try to remember to flip the roast two or three times while cooking to distribute the juices over the meat. If you don't, no worries; it will still taste good.

3 At 6 hours, remove the roast and shred it with two forks. Return the meat to the juices and mix to combine.

4 Place 2 slices of Swiss cheese on each roll, top with the shredded beef and pepperoncini mixture, then garnish with the giardiniera. Ladle out the remaining broth and serve on the side for dipping.

Cook's Notes | If you're not familiar with pepperoncini, they're not hot peppers, in spite of their appearance. They are juicy, sweet, and mild peppers, but some folks who are sensitive to heat might find them to be zesty. You can reduce the amount to 8 ounces or use only the juice from the jar to get the flavor and liquid with a little less of the actual pepper. The level of heat varies by brand or batch, so taste test before adding.

Giardiniera are Italian pickled vegetables usually found in the international food aisle or with sandwich condiments. Cauliflower, carrots, bell pepper, olives, and onion are common ingredients.

Fancy-Pants Sloppy Joes

This grown-up version of a childhood favorite is a far cry from the typical school lunch or the kind you get in a can. Even so, kids love these. The base is still a sweetened tomato sauce (basically good old ketchup) but with an extra kick of mustard and special seasonings and some hidden veggies because I love to sneak those in whenever I can.

An adult sloppy Joe requires a well-developed sauce that has simmered a while to marry the flavors. So although you can technically throw the mixture together in just 20 minutes, it tastes best after about 45 minutes—or even the next day. Using lean ground beef means you don't need to drain between additions. This saucy recipe can be hard to eat as an actual sandwich: I highly recommend serving them open face with a fork and knife.

PREP TIME | 10 minutes   **COOK TIME** | 50 minutes   **MAKES** | 4 sandwiches

- 2 teaspoons vegetable oil
- 1 pound 90% lean ground beef
- 1 cup chopped green bell pepper
- ¼ cup chopped white onion
- 2 garlic cloves, minced
- ¾ cup ketchup
- 2 tablespoons firmly packed light brown sugar
- 1 tablespoon red wine vinegar
- 1 tablespoon Worcestershire sauce
- 2 teaspoons yellow mustard
- ½ teaspoon kosher salt
- ½ teaspoon ground white pepper
- 4 potato or sesame hamburger buns

1 Heat the oil in a large skillet over medium-high heat. Add the beef, bell pepper, onion, and garlic, breaking apart the pieces of beef as it cooks. Cook until the onion softens and the meat is browned. If there's any liquid in the skillet, don't worry, it will absorb into the sauce.

2 Stir in the ketchup, sugar, vinegar, Worcestershire, mustard, salt, and pepper. Reduce the heat to low. Simmer, uncovered, for at least 10 and up to 45 minutes to allow the flavors to blend.

3 When ready to eat, spoon the beef sauce over hamburger buns and serve open face.

Cook's Note | This base recipe can be modified for every family. **Here are a few fun variations:**

- Add 2 tablespoons diced jalapeño to the ground beef mix or sprinkle a few jalapeño slices on top. Or use ½ teaspoon crushed red pepper flakes or Aleppo peppers for a different spice profile.
- Use pickles or pickled banana peppers as a topper.
- Add ½ cup cooked crumbled bacon or cooked crumbled Italian sausage to the mix.
- Bump up the veggie quotient with ½ cup grated carrots or parsnip. Corn is a good match for these flavors, too.
- Stir in ½ cup of your favorite cheese or add some on top.

Roast Beef Sandwiches with Creamy Horseradish Sauce

Let someone else cook the beef for this recipe while you focus on the all-important accompaniment of caramelized onions. All too often, people sauté onions and call them caramelized, but these are two very different methods of cooking. Sautéing keeps the signature onion flavor and aroma, while caramelizing transforms them into a sweet, deep amber deliciousness that doesn't really resemble onions much at all.

Zesty horseradish sauce completes the balance of sweet, umami, and slightly salty flavors. Serve these on small slider rolls to make the ultimate roast beef sandwiches. Add au jus for a French dip.

PREP TIME | 10 minutes   **COOK TIME** | 40 minutes   **MAKES** | 2 sandwiches or 8 sliders

1 tablespoon unsalted butter

2 large sweet onions, peeled and thinly sliced, then cut into strips

1 teaspoon sugar
Dash of kosher salt

2 large brioche buns or 8 slider rolls

⅓ cup Creamy Horseradish Sauce (page 132)

½ pound rare roast beef from the deli

1 Melt the butter in a large skillet over medium-low heat. Add the onions, sugar, and salt, and toss to coat. Cook for 35 to 40 minutes, tossing every 5 to 10 minutes, or until the onions are translucent and the color of caramel. Remember that slow and steady wins the race. If you start smelling the distinct aroma of sautéed onions, lower the heat.

2 When the onions are ready, cut the rolls and toast the insides only. Slather with the horseradish sauce, then drape thin slices of roast beef on top. Finish with the caramelized onions and the other half of the bun and serve.

BOVINE
Specials

Celebratory events are always marked by special foods. For many of us, beef is a top choice for a fancy meal. Some of these classic recipes happen to be among the easiest of beef preparations, yet home cooks are often intimidated by the pressure to get it right with a pricey cut of meat.

The good news is that the only way you can hurt most of these recipes is by overcooking them. Overcooking might make the meat a little chewy, but the cuts are so tender, even that won't make them taste bad. You've got this!

Herbed Beef Tenderloin with Sautéed Mushrooms

A tenderloin is a roast for special occasions where you're feeding a crowd and don't want to buy everyone their own filet mignon. It's an expensive cut, so there's a certain amount of stress in committing it to the oven, but I'm here to tell you that it's not rocket science. Probably the most time-consuming part is trimming and tying the roast, which you can usually have the butcher do for you. That may cost a dollar or so more per pound but will save you time and stress in the kitchen.

I don't recommend serving this particular cut at anything above medium doneness because the fibers shrink so much that this naturally tender cut starts to get dry and chewy. But at rare or medium rare, it can be sliced with a spoon. I like serving it with Fresh Herb Sauce (page 133), Tangy Steakhouse Steak Sauce (page 133), or Creamy Horseradish Sauce (page 132).

PREP TIME | 30 minutes   COOK TIME | 1 hour   SERVES | 8

1 tablespoon dried oregano
1 tablespoon dried parsley
1 tablespoon dried thyme
1 tablespoon garlic powder
1 tablespoon onion powder
1 tablespoon kosher salt
1 teaspoon coarsely ground black pepper
2 teaspoons dry mustard
4–5 pounds beef tenderloin, trimmed and tied

Cook's Note | Silver skin is a tough connective tissue found on certain cuts of beef. It doesn't break down during the cooking process, so for best results, it should be removed with a sharp knife before cooking. Simply slide the knife under the silver skin and carefully slice it off.

1 Combine the oregano, parsley, thyme, garlic powder, onion powder, salt, pepper, and dry mustard in a small bowl.

2 Rub the spice blend evenly over the whole roast, then place it on a rimmed baking sheet or roasting pan. Set aside at room temperature for 20 to 30 minutes to allow the spice mixture to adhere to the roast.

3 Preheat the oven to 450°F (230°C). Roast for 15 minutes, then reduce heat to 325°F (170°C). Continue to roast for 12 to 15 minutes per pound, or until the internal temperature reaches 125°F (52°C) for rare (this accounts for carryover cooking). The exact cooking time will depend on the size of your roast and desired degree of doneness. Use a meat thermometer to get it just right. (See Degrees of Doneness, page 16.)

4 Allow to rest for 10 to 15 minutes before slicing.

Sautéed Mushrooms

Mushrooms gain flavor when cooked down at a slow pace. They keep a little snap but reduce in size. For an added element of flavor, splash them with sherry or marsala.

4 cups sliced white mushrooms
2 tablespoons salted butter
2 teaspoons fresh thyme leaves
2 tablespoons sherry or marsala (optional)

1 Heat a large skillet over medium heat. Add the mushrooms to the dry skillet. Cook over medium heat for 10 to 15 minutes, stirring periodically, until the mushrooms brown, become fragrant, and reduce in size by about half.

2 Reduce the heat to low and add the butter and thyme. Stir until the butter is melted and well combined with the mushrooms. Add the sherry, if using, right before serving.

3 These mushrooms can be stored in the refrigerator for up to 5 days.

Mushroom-Crusted Ribeye with Balsamic Glaze

Many fine steakhouses offer a porcini-crusted Delmonico or mushroom-rubbed ribeye. While the name sounds fancy and the price usually matches, the execution is rather easy. It starts with a rub of dehydrated mushrooms, salt, red pepper flakes, and sugar that sits on the dry beef for about an hour. The salt pulls out the meat's natural juices to create a paste, and the sugar binds it together to make a crust when the meat is added to the hot skillet. The trick is to sear at a high enough temperature to cook the steak and to create a bark without burning it or setting off the smoke detectors.

A finishing touch of a balsamic reduction balances the heat of the red pepper flakes. This is one of my favorite "wow" dishes and delightfully simple to prepare.

PREP TIME | 10 minutes active, 45 minutes resting
COOK TIME | 12 minutes **SERVES** | 4

1 ounce dried mushrooms

1 tablespoon kosher salt

1 teaspoon red pepper flakes

1 teaspoon sugar

4 ribeye steaks, about 1½ inches thick, tied around the girth (see page 123)

1 teaspoon vegetable oil

½ cup Balsamic Glaze (page 134)

1. Place the dried mushrooms, salt, red pepper flakes, and sugar in the bowl of a small food processor and pulse to a uniform powder. Let the dust settle before opening.

2. Dab the steaks dry with a paper towel, then rub both sides with the dry rub. Set in the refrigerator for 45 minutes.

3. To cook, heat the oil in a large skillet over medium-high heat. Add the steak to the hot skillet and allow to cook for a total of 10 minutes, turning each side twice, for medium-rare doneness (135°F/57°C). Depending on the size of your steaks and the skillet, you may have to work in two batches. If that's the case, place the cooked steaks in a warm oven or tent them with aluminum foil while you cook the remaining ones. Allow to rest for at least 5 minutes.

4. Before serving, drizzle with the balsamic glaze.

> **Cook's Note** | Dried mushrooms are usually sold in small packets of 1 or 2 ounces in the produce section. Several varieties are available, but porcini is my favorite.

Crusted Bone-In Prime Rib

A bone-in prime rib (also called a standing rib roast) is perhaps the most impressive of beef roasts, with its handle of bone attached to a big piece of tender, well-marbled meat. This pricey cut is best served rare with a simple, flavorful bark and a side of Creamy Horseradish Sauce (page 132).

PREP TIME | 15 minutes active; 20 minutes resting
COOK TIME | 3 hours   **SERVES** | 8

2 tablespoons kosher salt

1 tablespoon freshly ground black pepper

1 tablespoon garlic powder

1 tablespoon onion powder

1 tablespoon minced fresh oregano

1 tablespoon minced fresh rosemary

1 tablespoon minced fresh thyme

10 pounds bone-in prime rib (4 ribs), tied

½ cup Dijon mustard

1 Arrange an oven rack in the lower-third position and preheat the oven to 450°F (230°C).

2 Mix the salt, pepper, garlic powder, onion powder, oregano, rosemary, and thyme in a small bowl.

3 Slather the roast with the mustard and then with the dry seasoning mix.

4 Place the roast, fat side up, in a large roasting pan. Roast in the oven for 20 minutes to form a nice crust. Lower the temperature to 325°F (170°C) and continue to roast for 15 minutes per pound, or until the roast reaches 120°F (49°C) on an instant-read thermometer.

5 Tent the roast with aluminum foil and let rest for 20 to 30 minutes before slicing.

> **Cook's Notes** | If you don't see a prime rib in the meat case, ask the butcher if there's one in the back. Estimate one bone for every two people.
>
> One of the key steps in cooking a prime rib is to tie it properly. Because of the high volume of marbling and the delicate fibers, it needs to be tied tautly for even cooking. Most butchers are happy to do this for you, but you can always do it yourself (see How to Tie Beef, facing page).

How to Tie Beef

While not always necessary, tying up a large piece of beef before cooking ensures that the meat retains its shape and cooks more evenly. With a recipe that calls for rolling up the meat, it keeps the roll tight and prevents any fillings from falling out.

Use cotton butcher's twine, also known as kitchen string, to tie your roast.

For individual cuts like a filet mignon, ribeye, or New York strip steak, tie around the girth, or "waist," of the meat to prevent spreading outward.

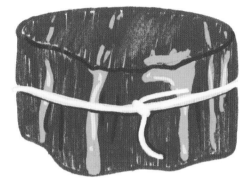

A roast is a little more challenging. Professional chefs use a method that calls for one long piece of string and a series of half-hitch knots (and right there, I've already lost half of you). That method allows you to adjust sections without having to untie the whole roast, but honestly, I find it easier just to use several individual pieces, tying them snugly, but not so tight that the meat is bulging around the string. Tie a piece of string every 1½ inches, spacing them evenly.

In the end, the roast should be tight, but the meat shouldn't be struggling against the twine or changing the shape. Remember, tying is to maintain a natural shape.

Don't forget to snip off the strings before carving your masterpiece!

Life-Changing Panfried Steak

Many people think that the only way to prepare steaks is on the grill, and while there is no shame in that game, never discount the panfried steak. It is a quick, effective, and supersimple way to achieve juicy steaks at home.

The trick, as it often is, is to create a good crust. Most seasonings or fresh herbs will burn in a smoking-hot pan, so other than a little salt and pepper, you add custom flavors at the end by way of a compound butter.

Transform this dish into bistro-style steak frites by serving the steak and butter over a bed of crunchy french fries.

PREP TIME | 5 minutes **COOK TIME** | 10 minutes **SERVES** | 2–4

- 2 (1½–2-inch-thick) New York strip steaks (1½–2 pounds)
- ½ teaspoon kosher salt
- ¼ teaspoon freshly ground black pepper
- 2 teaspoons vegetable oil (optional; see step 2)
- 2–3 tablespoons Maître d'Hôtel butter (page 126)

1 Season both sides of the steaks with the salt and pepper.

2 Heat a nonstick or cast-iron skillet over medium-high heat until the surface is nearly smoking. If using a regular skillet, add the oil. Add the steaks, allowing 1 inch between them. Cook them separately if necessary. Sear on each side for 3 to 4 minutes (6 to 8 minutes total), or until they develop a deep brown crust and register 125°F (52°C) for rare or 145°F (63°C) for medium.

3 Transfer to a cutting board and allow to rest for 4 to 5 minutes. When plated, top with a tablespoon of the butter, allowing the heat from the steak to soften the butter.

Cook's Note | Cooking times vary by the thickness of the overall cut. If your steak is 2 inches thick, the outside will burn by the time the inside reaches medium doneness. Either serve thicker steaks at rare, or, if you like a more well-cooked steak, transfer it to an oven preheated at 300°F (150°C) for about 5 minutes to finish cooking to your desired degree of doneness (see page 16).

Compound Butters

My husband jokes that bread is just a socially acceptable way to get butter into my mouth. It comes as no surprise that I love making compound, or flavored, butters. They are an easy way to elevate any meal and, if you have the time, can be piped into fun shapes. Butter is a sponge that takes on flavors and scents, so letting flavored butter sit only amplifies the intensity.

To make a compound butter, mix herbs and seasonings into softened butter. It really is that simple! Cover any leftovers tightly—butter will absorb other flavors if left uncovered—and store in the refrigerator for up to 1 week.

Maître d'Hôtel

- ½ cup unsalted butter, softened
- 1 teaspoon Dijon mustard
- ½ teaspoon lemon zest
- ½ teaspoon kosher salt
- 1 tablespoon finely minced flat-leaf parsley

Lime & Chile

- ½ cup salted butter, softened
- ¼ teaspoon ancho chile powder
- 1 teaspoon lime zest

Cranberry

- ½ cup salted butter, softened
- ¼ cup finely chopped dried cranberries

Maple Bacon

- ½ cup unsalted butter, softened
- ¼ cup crumbled crispy cooked bacon
- 1 teaspoon maple syrup

Hot Honey

- ½ cup salted butter
- 2 teaspoons hot sauce
- 2 tablespoons honey

Miso Scallion

- ½ cup unsalted butter
- 2 tablespoons miso paste
- 1 scallion, charred and thinly sliced
- ¼ teaspoon coarsely ground black pepper

Easier Beef Burgundy

Beef Burgundy, or Boeuf Bourguignon, the rich French dish made famous by Julia Child, is not an everyday meal, but it is well worth the time and effort to make it. The first time I tried it, I had to read the confusing directions several times and the dish still didn't turn out as planned. Eventually I figured out ways to cut corners without losing any flavor.

The main cooking techniques are (1) browning the meat to add to the richness of the sauce and (2) braising it for hours over low heat to achieve a meltingly tender texture. The lengthy cooking time allows layers of flavor to develop and mellow, so that each bite has dimension.

PREP TIME | 45 minutes   **COOK TIME** | 4 hours   **SERVES** | 8

1½ pounds chuck roast, cut into 2-inch pieces

2 tablespoons cornstarch

1 tablespoon extra-virgin olive oil

7 strips thick-cut bacon, cut into ½-inch pieces

1 cup fresh pearl onions, peeled

¾ cup diced carrots

3 garlic cloves, thinly sliced

3 cups dry red wine

2 tablespoons tomato paste

3 cups low-sodium beef broth, plus more as needed

10–12 sprigs fresh herbs, tied into a bouquet garni (see Cook's Notes, page 128)

2 bay leaves

3 tablespoons unsalted butter

2½ cups halved or quartered white mushrooms

Pasta, mashed potatoes, or rice, for serving

1 Arrange an oven rack in the lower-third position and preheat the oven to 275°F (135°C).

2 In a large bowl, toss the beef with the cornstarch to coat. Set aside.

3 Heat the oil in a large Dutch oven over medium-high heat. Add the bacon, cooking until browned and crispy, 8 to 10 minutes. Remove with a slotted spoon to a paper towel–lined plate. Set aside.

4 In the same pot, add the beef, working in two batches. Brown on all sides, 7 to 8 minutes total, then transfer to a clean bowl. Repeat with the next batch and set aside.

5 In the same pot, without wiping it out, add the onions, carrots, and garlic, tossing to coat in the rendered bacon grease and browned bits. Cook until lightly browned and starting to soften, 6 to 7 minutes. Remove with a slotted spoon to a bowl and set aside.

6 Reduce the heat to low. At this point there should be little to no oil or grease pooling if you tip the pot to one side, but if there is, spoon it out. Pour the wine into the pot and scrape up the browned bits on the bottom. Keeping the pot on low heat, whisk in the tomato paste, then the broth.

7 Return the beef, bacon, and cooked vegetables to the pot and add the bouquet garni and bay leaves. There should be enough liquid to fully cover the meat and vegetables. If not, add just enough additional broth to do so.

8 Cover the pot and bake for 3 to 4 hours, or until the beef falls apart when split with a fork. If there is any fat on top, skim it off with a spoon before stirring. Remove and discard the bouquet garni and bay leaves. Cover the pot.

Continued on next page

9 Melt the butter in a medium skillet over medium heat. Add the mushrooms and cook until they reduce in size by a third. Stir the mushrooms into the beef mixture.

10 Serve over pasta, mashed potatoes, or rice.

Cook's Notes | A bouquet garni eliminates the need to sieve the gravy to remove the herbs. You can use any combination of herbs, but I find a "poultry pack" of thyme, rosemary, and sage to be the easiest. Tie the herbs into a pouch using a large square of cheesecloth and some kitchen twine. If you don't have cheesecloth, you will need to remove the meat and vegetables with a slotted spoon, then strain the liquid through a colander or sieve to separate out the herb bits and stems to have a smooth sauce.

Beef Burgundy isn't quick or easy to make, but it's perfect for preparing ahead of time. In fact, Julia Child recommended that it be made the day before and reheated to allow flavors to further develop. If you do this, wait to add the mushrooms until reheating so they keep their unique texture. Warm the sauce in a large Dutch oven over medium heat, until evenly heated.

Freezer Friendly: Freeze leftovers in an airtight container for up to 3 months.

Braised Short Ribs

Short ribs are one of those funny things that many cooks are scared to make at home. A moist heat over a long period of time is the best way to break down the fibers and get maximum potential out of the supertender and ribbon-marbled meat. Serve them bone-in over polenta, mashed potatoes, egg noodles, or rice. Shred the leftover meat off the bone for dressing up a grilled cheese sandwich or quesadilla, mixing into soup, or piling on top of a burger or breakfast sandwich.

When buying bone-in short ribs, look for thick, meaty pieces with good marbling on intramuscular meat. Some butchers might label them as "English cut," which refers to a smaller piece, 2 to 3 inches long, with a thick layer of meat on the bone. Plan for two or three bones per person depending on size.

PREP TIME | 30 minutes   **COOK TIME** | 4 hours 30 minutes   **SERVES** | 4 (2 ribs per person)

½ cup all-purpose flour

1 teaspoon coarse sea salt

¼ teaspoon freshly ground black pepper

8 bone-in short ribs

2 teaspoons vegetable oil

4–5 strips center-cut bacon, cut into 1-inch pieces

4 cups low-sodium beef broth

2 cups dry red wine

3 tablespoons tomato paste

1 white onion, quartered

2 ribs celery, cut into 3-inch pieces

3 carrots, cut into 2-inch pieces

4 garlic cloves, peeled and lightly smashed

2–3 sprigs flat-leaf parsley

2–3 sprigs fresh rosemary

2–3 sprigs fresh sage

2–3 sprigs fresh thyme

2 bay leaves

1 tablespoon cornstarch

2 tablespoons cold water

Mashed potatoes, polenta, pasta, or rice, for serving

1. Arrange an oven rack in the lower-third position and preheat the oven to 300°F (150°C).

2. Combine the flour, salt, and pepper in a large bowl. Toss with the short ribs, tapping off the excess flour. Set aside.

3. Heat 1 teaspoon of the oil in a large Dutch oven or enamel pot over high heat. Add the bacon. Cook until crispy. Using a slotted spoon, transfer the bacon to a paper towel–lined plate, leaving the fat in the pot.

4. Reduce the heat to medium and add the short ribs, working in batches of two or three. Brown well on all sides. If needed, add the remaining 1 teaspoon oil to prevent sticking. Be careful not to burn the bacon fat or the flour on the ribs. Transfer the ribs to a plate. Remove all remaining grease from the pot and wipe it clean with a paper towel held with tongs.

5. Return the short ribs to the pot. Cover them with the broth, wine, and 2 tablespoons of the tomato paste, stirring to combine. Return the cooked bacon and add the onion, celery, carrot, garlic, parsley, rosemary, sage, thyme, and bay leaves to the pot. Bring the mixture to a low simmer, then cover and place in the bottom third of the oven. Braise for 3 hours and 30 minutes, or until meat starts to separate from the bone.

6. Carefully transfer the short ribs to a plate. Place a fine-mesh colander over a heatproof fat skimmer. Pour the pot liquid through the colander, discarding all solids. Allow the liquid to sit for a moment, then skim off the fat and grease.

7 Pour the strained liquid into a medium saucepan and bring to a boil. Whisk in the remaining 1 tablespoon tomato paste. Allow to reduce by about one-third, approximately 5 minutes.

8 Whisk the cornstarch and water in a small bowl and add this paste to the saucepan, whisking well. The gravy should thicken immediately. Remove the pan from the heat.

9 Place the short ribs over the mashed potatoes, polenta, pasta, or rice, and top with the sauce.

Cook's Note | This dish is fancy enough for a dinner party and perfect for making ahead. If doing so, instead of using a heatproof fat skimmer, let the entire dish cool after being removed from the oven. The fat will solidify and be easy to remove as a solid piece. From there, strain the gravy, reheat the ribs in the oven for 10 minutes at 350°F (180°C), then continue to make the sauce.

Sauce on the Side

A perfectly cooked steak, juicy hamburger, or piled-high sandwich can always be made a tad tastier with the right condiment. These easy-to-make sauces will elevate any dish.

Creamy Horseradish Sauce

Creamy horseradish is the best accompaniment for almost any steak or beef sandwich. For best results, allow it to sit for 2 hours or more before serving. It can be made up to 48 hours in advance but will need a quick stir before serving.

Makes 1 cup

- 2 tablespoons prepared horseradish
- 1 cup sour cream
- 2 tablespoons apple cider vinegar
- 2 tablespoons Worcestershire sauce
- ½ teaspoon kosher salt
- 1 tablespoon chopped fresh chives

1 Press the horseradish through a small fine-mesh sieve with the back of a spoon to remove as much liquid as possible. Mix the horseradish with the sour cream, vinegar, Worcestershire, salt, and chives in a small bowl until well combined.

2 Cover and chill for at least 2 and up to 48 hours before serving. The sauce can be stored in the refrigerator for up to 1 week.

Quick Garlic Aioli

This "cheater's aioli" uses prepared mayo as a base instead of olive oil to produce nearly the same results. It is delicious slathered on any sandwich with beef (or chicken) and can be used as a dip for french fries and other sides.

Makes 1 cup

- 3 cloves garlic, roughly chopped
- 1 cup mayonnaise, preferably one made with olive oil
- 2 teaspoons lemon juice
  Pinch of kosher salt

Pulse the garlic in a food processor until finely minced. Add the mayonnaise, lemon juice, and salt, and pulse until smooth. Chill for at least 1 hour before using to let the flavors marry. Store in the refrigerator for up to 1 week.

Tangy Steakhouse Steak Sauce

Most signature steak sauces include an element of zing, be it hot sauce, anchovies, or horseradish, as with this version. The horseradish can be adjusted or omitted as you wish, or you can experiment with other variations.

Makes ¾ cup

- ½ cup ketchup
- 1 tablespoon Dijon mustard
- 3 tablespoons Worcestershire sauce
- 2 tablespoons firmly packed light brown sugar
- 1 tablespoon apple cider vinegar
- 1–3 teaspoons prepared horseradish, drained
- ¼ teaspoon celery salt
- ¼ teaspoon garlic powder
- ¼ teaspoon onion powder

Whisk the ketchup and mustard in a small bowl until smooth. Add the Worcestershire, sugar, vinegar, horseradish, celery salt, garlic powder, and onion powder, and whisk to combine thoroughly. The sauce can be enjoyed right after mixing, but the flavor will improve if allowed to sit for a few hours. Cover and refrigerate until ready to serve. The sauce can be stored for up to 1 week.

Fresh Herb Sauce

This bright and colorful sauce is great for beef, but it also enhances chicken, pork, and grilled vegetables. If you don't have a small food processor, mincing the ingredients by hand will work fine. The sauce is meant to be slightly chunky, not a smooth blend.

Makes ¾ cup

- 1 small shallot, coarsely chopped
- 1 garlic clove, coarsely chopped
- ⅓ cup fresh mint leaves, packed
- ⅓ cup fresh flat-leaf parsley leaves, packed
- 1 tablespoon capers, drained and rinsed
- 1 teaspoon kosher salt
- 1 teaspoon lemon zest
  Juice from 1 lemon (about 3 tablespoons)
- ½ teaspoon freshly ground black pepper
- ⅓ cup extra-virgin olive oil

Combine the shallot and garlic in a small food processor. Pulse several times to mince. Add the mint, parsley, capers, salt, lemon zest, lemon juice, and pepper. Pulse until all the greens are coarsely chopped. Pour in the oil and pulse several more times until a thick sauce forms. Serve at room temperature. This can be made up to 1 day in advance and stored, covered, for up to 3 days.

Balsamic Glaze

Tart vinegar caramelizes to a sweet, sticky syrup that balances its acidic flavors. You can buy a reduction of balsamic vinegar for a pretty penny, but making it at home is supercheap, and I recommend having some on hand at all times. It's an excellent condiment for beef and other meats, goes well with roasted or grilled veggies, and gives a lively boost to grain-based dishes and salads.

Makes ¾ cup

- 1 cup balsamic vinegar
- 1 tablespoon firmly packed light brown sugar
- Dash of fine sea salt

Combine the vinegar and sugar in a small saucepan over low heat. Simmer until reduced in volume by half, about 15 minutes, stirring every few minutes. Stir in the salt, then remove the pan from the heat. The mixture will not appear thick, but it will thicken and turn glossy as it cools. It should coat the back of a spoon.

Store refrigerated for up to 1 month. Because the chilled sauce will be thick and syrupy, I suggest allowing it to sit at room temperature for 10 to 15 minutes before drizzling on your favorite foods.

METRIC CONVERSIONS

Unless you have finely calibrated measuring equipment, conversions between US and metric measurements will be somewhat inexact. It's important to convert the measurements for all of the ingredients in a recipe to maintain the same proportions as the original.

WEIGHT

To convert	to	multiply
ounces	grams	ounces by 28.35
pounds	grams	pounds by 453.5
pounds	kilograms	pounds by 0.45

US	Metric	US	Metric	US	Metric
0.035 ounce	1 gram	1½ ounces	40 grams	5 ounces	140 grams
¼ ounce	7 grams	1¾ ounces	50 grams	8 ounces	228 grams
½ ounce	14 grams	2½ ounces	70 grams	8¾ ounces	250 grams
1 ounce	28 grams	3½ ounces	100 grams	10 ounces	280 grams
1¼ ounces	35 grams	4 ounces	113 grams	15 ounces	425 gram
				16 ounces (1 pound)	454 grams

VOLUME

To convert	to	multiply
teaspoons	milliliters	teaspoons by 4.93
tablespoons	milliliters	tablespoons by 14.79
fluid ounces	milliliters	fluid ounces by 29.57
cups	milliliters	cups by 236.59
cups	liters	cups by 0.24
pints	milliliters	pints by 473.18
pints	liters	pints by 0.473
quarts	milliliters	quarts by 946.36
quarts	liters	quarts by 0.946
gallons	liters	gallons by 3.785

US	Metric
1 teaspoon	5 milliliters
1 tablespoon	15 milliliters
¼ cup	60 milliliters
½ cup	120 milliliters
1 cup	240 milliliters
1¼ cups	300 milliliters
1½ cups	355 milliliters
2 cups	480 milliliters
2½ cups	600 milliliters
3 cups	710 milliliters
4 cups (1 quart)	0.95 liter
4 quarts (1 gallon)	3.8 liters

ACKNOWLEDGMENTS

The saying "it takes a village" is true not only for raising children, but also for writing books, especially cookbooks. A big thank you to:

Everyone at the Certified Angus Beef brand, especially Margaret Coleman, Chef Michael Ollier, Tony Biggs, Melissa Brewer, and Beth Barner, who let me bounce around ideas and provided feedback and support from the very beginning.

Debbie Blythe-Lyons, my favorite female cattle rancher, and her family for their knowledge of and passion for all things cattle.

Alice Kimball Schott and Beth Merchant from Bowman's Butcher Shop in Aberdeen, Maryland, for their expertise on processing and butchering.

And my recipe testers, who also indulged in days upon days of eating delicious beefy meals: Debra and Edward Fasano; Justin and Jen Eames; Kristen Wellock and family; Sandra and Ben Formicola; Dana, Bob, Addie, and Alex Young; Jaclyn Fasano and Donald DeSantis; Pat Stabile and family; Nathalie Magiera and family; Kathy Henderberg and family; Donna and Gary Goldstein; and Brandon and Jennifer Ring.

INDEX

Page numbers in **bold** indicate charts.

ENJOY EASY, DELICIOUS MEALS
with More Cookbooks from Storey

Build-a-Bowl
by Nicki Sizemore

With this fuss-free formula, you can create 77 delicious and nourishing grain bowls for any meal of the day. Countless options for customizing help you suit individual diets and tastes.

The Make-Ahead Sauce Solution
by Elisabeth Bailey

Transform your weeknight cooking with these 62 easy, make-ahead, freezer-friendly sauces. From All-American Barbecue to Chorizo Garlic, and Pumpkin Coconut Cream to Gorgonzola-Chive Butter, there's something here for everyone.

Winner! Winner! Chicken Dinner
by Stacie Billis

This cookbook offers more than 50 irresistible chicken dishes, from Sheet Pan Shwarma to Green and White Chicken Chili, plus easy instructions for basic chicken-cooking techniques, including braising, roasting, grilling, and slow cooking.